WHEN
FAITH
STEALS
HOME

WHEN FAITH STEALS HOME

by
Duane G. Sandul

Logos International
Plainfield, New Jersey

Scripture verses marked TLB are taken
from The Living Bible, copyright 1971 by
Tyndale House Publishers, Wheaton, Ill.
Used by permission.

Scripture verses marked RSV are taken
from the Revised Standard Version of the
Bible, copyrighted 1946, 1952, © 1971,
1973. Used by permission.

About the Author

Duane G. Sandul launched his newspaper career in 1965 as a sportswriter before he turned to general news in 1970, becoming a specialist in reporting on the criminal justice system. He presently is a reporter and religion editor for the San Mateo *Times*, a suburban newspaper, located south of San Francisco. Duane and his wife, Diana, have two sons, Glenn and Paul, and they live in San Jose. They attend church in Milpitas, California.

Acknowledgments

Learning how dozens of major-league baseball players rely on the Lord Jesus to endure the ups and downs of a grueling, challenging season became a compelling mission for me—one which took most of the 1979 season for exploring, observing and interviewing more than 100 Christian athletes.

Their stories and their faith are revealing.

Acknowledgments must start with the players themselves. All but two players consented to interviews; only a few Christian players were not interviewed—those who were on the disabled list and not traveling with their respective teams during the interviews.

I extend my appreciation to press information officers, Stu Smith of the San Francisco Giants and Carl Finley of the Oakland A's, both of whom provided passes for countless games, and to Dick Draper, an award-winning, sensitive sportswriter for the San Mateo *Times* who helped in so many ways.

My wife, Diana Sandul, spent hours transcribing each of the taped interviews, a feat which enabled the accurate quotation of each of the players. Christopher Robinson, a student at Seattle Pacific, and B. Randle Helton, a pastor at King's Way Community Church in San Mateo, California, contributed to my writing immensely with their constructive and pointed criticisms and suggestions along the way.

But most of all, an acknowledgment goes to the Lord Jesus, who is working wonders in the major leagues!

Introduction

There's more to America's national pastime than batting averages and league standings.

There is love. There are fulfilled lives that were once dominated by loneliness and emptiness. There is happiness which material success fails to bring. There is strength to resist temptation. There is security in a profession where security is felt to be nonexistent. There is faith in action.

A Christian revolution is sweeping major-league baseball with a direct impact among the 650 players on 26 teams. The words, "Jesus Christ," were once mentioned only in locker room profanity, but now they have become sacred because they comprise the name of a dominating figure in the lives of nearly one of every five players.

Dozens more are searching; many attend Baseball Chapel services on Sundays preceding games. Baseball Chapel, Inc., was founded in 1973 by former Detroit sportswriter Watson

Spoelstra to provide Sunday chapel services at all major-league ballparks. Baseball Chapel arranges for regional representatives to schedule speakers at the chapel services. Several players attribute their faith or rededication to the Lord to this program.

Players are discovering that their strength lies not in bats or arms or bodies but in a personal relationship with Jesus Christ. But yet, national attention still focuses on the salary demands, indiscretions and locker room bickering involving a minority of players. Popular books and sporting pages across the nation seemingly ignore the spiritual awakening which is reshaping the lives of players, and, ultimately, the game itself.

America, perhaps like no other country in the world, practically worships its athletes, turning professional sports into a form of idolatry. Impressionable youngsters are treated by the national press to many features about ballplayers, but they never see how Jesus Christ helps many players, enabling them to focus on God during the peaks and valleys of baseball and life.

Some of baseball's foremost players have been born again, many of them after reaching national acclaim for their on-the-field successes. Others players have nurtured their lifelong faith and matured with it.

The Christian revival in baseball is the story

of Mike Schmidt, Joe Rudi, Gene Tenace and Bill Russell becoming more loving husbands and fathers. It is the story of Tommy John, Rico Carty, Adrian Devine, George Foster, Nolan Ryan, Steve Garvey and others invoking God's power through their steadfastness in faith.

It is the story of Bill Madlock, Bob Watson, Gary Lavelle, Ken Singleton and others finding that Jesus satisfies the relentless search for genuine happiness. It is the story of several single players' reliance on the Lord to help them combat sexual temptations.

It is the story of Andre Thornton, in a time of personal sorrow over the death of his wife and daughter, praising the Lord and giving strength to those who had intended to console him. It is the story of Jack Brohamer coming to the Lord in the aftermath of a tragic fire which killed three relatives.

It is the unfolding story of how many players are learning to put Jesus Christ first in their lives, ahead of the glamour and material rewards of baseball.

It is the story of faith in action—Don Baylor for cystic fibrosis, Chris Speier for the Pro-Life Movement, Garry Maddox for child-guidance clinics and Bill Robinson for rheumatic diseases.

When Faith Steals Home traces the lives of players on every major-league team in 1979, showing how the Christian faith has made an enormous impact in professional baseball. Some of the featured players, including Nolan Ryan, Dave Goltz, John Denny, and Adrian Devine, were traded or signed contracts with new teams after the 1979 season.

Some books on baseball focus on how a few players act off the field, painting them as wild playboys who are more interested in women, booze and money than the game itself. Indeed, there are players, as there are people in any walk of life, who turn to immoral activities for pleasure.

But there is a trend in major-league baseball that is contrary to that which is being sensationalized. More and more players, admitting their sins and their weaknesses, are turning to the Lord Jesus to guide their lives. He provides them with a rulebook for living.

At the heart of the spiritual renewal in baseball is a Sunday chapel service started in 1973 by Baseball Chapel. Speakers go to clubhouses each Sunday to share the Lord with players.

There are several reasons why a growing number of players are turning to Jesus Christ. The foremost include:

1. Material rewards don't fill the void in a life without the Lord.

2. A sports-crazed society tends to rob players of their individuality, causing many of

them to search for deeper meaning in life.

3. Loneliness is rampant among ballplayers. Long stretches away from their wives and families can be testing periods and these trips also provide more free time than many players can handle.

4. Security is nonexistent. A player's status is based on performance. Last year's statistics don't count. Consequently, many players feel insecure, despite their huge salaries. This insecurity manifests itself in many ways.

There are also noticeable differences between many Christian players and their nonbelieving associates. They include:

1. Most Christian players are secure in their athletic profession, treating baseball as a game, an occupation, a dramatic performance. They realize God has a precise plan for their lives in and out of baseball.

2. Christian players want to win as much as anyone, but most have the ability to turn the pressure to win over to the Lord.

3. Christian players seem more open, loving, tolerant and less likely to be troubled by worries or tensions created by the game.

Players turning to the Lord Jesus realize that the macho image of baseball players is outdated. Some players avoid public professions of their faith, fearing that their lives, already open to public inspection, may be further put under microscopic scrutiny by a nation which by and large fails to grasp the Lord's love and forgiveness.

Even so, there is a mushrooming trend toward sports evangelism, including an annual conference which prepares players to share their faith in Jesus Christ with fans and friends.

When Faith Steals Home shares how players draw upon their Christian faith to help them deal with sexual temptations, maintain family lives, handle tragedies, deal with their playboy image, and handle winning, losing, trades, and their careers in general.

WHEN
FAITH
STEALS
HOME

chapter one

When a team like the Cleveland Indians has to sport a losing history, fans follow players rather than the club. Though the squad may become mired in the basement of the American League's strong Eastern Division, steady fans cheer for the Indian or Indians who are playing best. If the team cannot win a pennant, hopefully a player will nab an individual honor, fans reason.

Andre Thornton is the shining light of the Indians—and one of the brightest stars of major-league baseball. His consistent performance and his uplifting Christian spirit bring a sparkle to Cleveland and ease the frustration of the inability to win a pennant since 1954. His unwavering faith serves as a model for players throughout baseball.

In the face of a tragic car accident on the Pennsylvania Turnpike which claimed the lives of his wife, Gertrude, and their two-year-old daughter, Theresa, on October 17, 1977, Andre Thornton stood calmly proclaiming God's glory.

Sportswriters couldn't understand it. He wasn't bitter. He didn't shake his fist skyward. He didn't sink into depression. Secular writers handled Andre Thornton the only way they knew how—they ignored his inspirational reaction.

Christians turned to Thornton with the same amazement but with perhaps a more understanding heart. But even many Christians marveled at how a man could actually live his faith in this manner. It is easy to talk about walking with God in the wake of adversity. It is quite another story to actually do so.

Thornton, a quiet man who was born on August 13, 1949, in Tuskegee, Alabama, could have copied Job of the Old Testament. He could have asked God, as Job did, "Don't just condemn me—tell me why you are doing it. Does it really seem right to you to oppress and despise me, a man you have made?" (Job 10:2, 3 TLB).

But Andre Thornton's faith didn't waver.

Speaking modestly in an impersonal, editorial "we," Thornton shared why he wasn't bitter and angry. "It is hard for people to understand how one can really trust in God and believe the Word. When God tells us He will never leave us or forsake us, it is true. In our times of trouble we can call upon Him and He will hear."

Many people persistently ask, "How can he do it?"

"I'm trusting in His Word," Thornton replies. "It is nothing other than His Word that we hold on to. The promise of His Word enables us to hold on and to go through a difficult time. And it is the same Word that will hold and keep others up this same way as they go through hard times.

"Whatever God allows to come about in our lives, He tells us that all things work for good for those who love Him. It was that understanding that enabled us to grow in marriage for seven years, and to rejoice in the Word. It enables us to hold on in a time where there seemingly is no comfort, but yet God is there."

Elihu told Job, "God is greater than man. Why should you fight against him just because he does not give account to you of what he does?" (Job 33:12, 13 TLB).

Thornton agrees. That's why he hasn't waged a fight to understand the tragedy in human terms.

"I don't think God is required to tell us why He does things," Thornton asserted. "I've seen the Lord bless many lives through what has happened, which may give us a little evidence of why He allowed it to occur. But God doesn't

3

come down and explain it to us. He doesn't have to.

"Through the type of tragedy we have had," Thornton said, continuing to shy away from first-person dialogue, "many people have become aware of the fact that we are Christians and how the Lord has been our strength through a time of sorrow. And He has given us an opportunity to witness for Him in the greatest of ways because He has illuminated the Word to our lives. We're thankful that Christians and non-Christians have gained strength through this."

Thornton finds solace in the Bible passage, "We are pressed on every side by troubles, but not crushed and broken. We are perplexed because we don't know why things happen as they do, but we don't give up and quit" (2 Cor. 4:8 TLB).

The same passage continues, "These troubles and sufferings of ours are, after all, quite small and won't last very long. Yet this short time of distress will result in God's richest blessing upon us forever and ever! So we do not look at what we can see right now, the troubles all around us, but we look forward to the joys in heaven which we have not yet seen. The troubles will soon be over, but the joys to come will last forever" (2 Cor. 4:17, 18 TLB).

For Andre Thornton, belief in God's Word

demands obedience—even in the face of tragedy.

"It is something we have no control over," Thornton said. "It is God's plan and we just have to learn to praise Him in it, and realize it is His will. I'm just thankful I knew Him and loved Him so I could give Him that much. I thank Him for His strength."

Thornton remained a widower, raising seven-year-old Andre, Jr., until November 4, 1978, when he married Gail Jones, the daughter of a preacher. Her sister married Pat Kelly of the Baltimore Orioles three months later. The Thorntons live in Chagrin Falls, Ohio.

Andre was the unanimous recipient of the "Danny Thompson Memorial Award" in 1978, presented annually by the Baseball Chapel for "exemplary Christian spirit in baseball." (The award was named for Danny Thompson who was a shortstop with the Minnesota Twins and Texas Rangers; he exhibited inspiring Christian strength during his long battle with leukemia. Thompson died in 1976. He played for four years with the knowledge of his disease.)

Thornton has a stocky build; he is six-feet-two inches tall and weighs 205 pounds. He surrendered his life to Jesus Christ while sitting in an army barracks at Fort Dix, New Jersey, weeks after he culminated an outstanding prep athletic career at Phoenixville High School in Pennsylvania. As a student, he starred in

5

baseball, basketball, and football.

The loneliness of being a soldier directed Thornton toward God. "I came to the realization that we are not worthy of the Lord. We're sinners. Without that realization, none of us can come to Him."

Like many young men in the war-torn late sixties, Thornton searched for a purpose in life. He refused, though, to let the drug culture or politics turn him sour on life or America. Instead, he searched for God.

"I saw that there are questions that need to be answered in our lives," Thornton recalled in an interview before a game in Oakland. "I needed to know where we're going, and the purpose of this life."

Turning to Christ, he learned the world cannot answer those questions.

"When we read in the Bible that through believing in Jesus Christ we have eternal life, that's the answer," Thornton asserted. "I was a sinner and unworthy of God. I had to come to Him the only way He's made available—through His Son, Jesus Christ."

So in the barracks of Fort Dix, Andre Thornton unceremoniously dropped to his knees and prayed for forgiveness. He gave the reins of his life to Jesus Christ.

The apostle John, in the Bible, explains it like this: "For God loved the world so much that he gave his only Son so that anyone who believes in him shall not perish but have eternal life. God did not send his Son into the world to condemn it, but to save it" (John 3:16, 17 TLB).

After his brief military stint, Thornton signed with the Philadelphia Phillies, fulfilling a dream nurtured since playing in a Babe Ruth World Series as a youngster. But success didn't develop easily for Thornton. He played in the minor leagues from 1967 through mid-1974 and was twice traded before Chicago made him their first baseman early in the 1974 season.

After two respectable seasons in which he hit .261 and .293 with a total of 28 homers, Thornton was traded to the Montreal Expos after the 1976 season began. In exchange, Chicago received pitcher Steve Renko and outfielder Larry Bittner. The Expos traded Thornton to Cleveland for pitcher Jackie Brown on December 10, 1976.

His first two seasons with Cleveland elevated Thornton to among the American League's most feared hitters. He walloped 28 homers in 1977, followed by 33 in 1978.

His life, though, has been centered in the Lord, not in baseball.

"My faith has been my mainstay all of my life," Thornton said. "The Holy Spirit guides and directs our lives. Life generates around our faith, not our faith around our life. We certainly

7

cannot live our lives as Christians as the Lord wants us to without allowing Him, through faith, to let the Holy Spirit guide and direct our paths. That's the key lesson as a Christian—to see that our lives are revolving around our faith in Christ."

Jesus told His apostles that He would send a Comforter: "He is the Holy Spirit, the Spirit who leads into all truth. The world at large cannot receive him, for it isn't looking for him and doesn't recognize him. But you do, for he lives with you now and some day [after the Ascension] shall be in you" (John 14:17 TLB).

Jesus said, "When the Holy Spirit, who is truth, comes, he shall guide you into all truth, for he will not be presenting his own ideas, but will be passing on to you what he has heard. He will tell you about the future" (John 16:13 TLB).

Andre Thornton draws upon the Holy Spirit to lift him in all aspects of his life, including the temptations which hound major-league players. "He keeps me afloat. Without Him, we would fall prey to this world and this flesh as easily as a man desiring a nice cold drink on a hot day."

Thornton's example has inspired Mike Paxton, a starting pitcher for the Indians. "I'm tickled to death to be with Cleveland, not just in a baseball capacity, but to be in contact with men like Andre and Rick Waits," said Paxton, cooling down after wind sprints before a game.

8

Paxton became one of Cleveland's most consistent pitchers after his trade from Boston in 1978, with a 12-11 record.

"Andre has been a tremendous influence on my life," said Paxton. "He is probably one of the most godly people I've ever known. His courage and his stand for the Lord are an inspiration."

Born September 3, 1953, Paxton converted to Christianity in junior high school. "I was the type of Christian who kept my faith hidden," he recalled with a chuckle. "Nobody else knew because I wasn't strong enough to share it."

After a respectable collegiate career at Memphis State University, the five-feet-eleven, 190-pound Paxton was drafted by the Red Sox organization. He pitched in only 47 minor-league games in two-plus seasons before his elevation to the major leagues in 1977. He won 10, lost 5 in his rookie season.

Paxton's Christian development paralleled his baseball development.

"There was a time when I wasn't sure whether playing baseball was the right job for me," Paxton recalled. "I just got down on my knees and prayed, 'Lord, if this is what you want me to do just let me do it.' It was up to Him."

Discouragement can trap any athlete striving for achievement. A player in the lineup every day always has tomorrow. But a starting pitcher has a performance only once every four, five or six days. Consecutive shellings by the opposition can leave one questioning his own abilities and his faith.

"Certainly I struggled during the first part of the 1979 season," Paxton asserted, adding knowingly, "no one said being a Christian was going to be easy. If it was easy, everybody in the world would want to do it. There are times when He is testing us to see whether we are with Him just when things are going good, or with Him when things are going bad. The Lord tests us to see how strong we really are. Things aren't going to go our way every time out. I've been shelled a number of times but that's not going to get me discouraged."

Conversely, a winning streak can cause a player to rely exclusively on his own abilities, slipping into the I-did-it syndrome.

"When that happens, He will bring you down to your knees every time," said Paxton. "And when He does, it just makes you say, 'Thank you, Lord, because I was getting away from you and you brought me back.' That's the joy a Christian can have when he is in continual fellowship with God."

Paxton and his wife, Julia, live in Germantown, Tennessee, with their infant son, Michael Joshua. "We continue to grow in the Lord together," Paxton said.

The material aspects of baseball have spoiled many players. But not Mike Paxton.

"I realize what a lot of people don't understand—there is more to this life than just sixty or seventy years on this earth. What we accumulate we're not going to take with us. We are formed from the dust, and that is where we are going to return. Whatever happens in between is really of no consequence as far as material things are concerned. What matters is whether we have our lives right with God. I feel that I do. I have peace, and I don't worry. I feel that if I do what He wants me to do and I try to live the best life I can, then He is going to take care of the material things. I do not have to worry about them. He will meet my needs."

In the Sermon on the Mount, when Jesus says that we cannot serve two masters—God and money—He explains, "My counsel is: Don't worry about things—food, drink, money, and clothes. For you already have life and a body— and they are far more important than what to eat and wear. Look at the birds! They don't worry about what to eat—they don't need to sow or reap or store up food—for your heavenly Father feeds them. And you are far more valuable to him than they are. Will all your worries add a single moment to your life?" (Matt. 6:25-27 TLB).

Rick Waits is another Cleveland pitcher who relinquished worries to the Lord as a prep athlete. But he stumbled because he tried to keep his faith separate from baseball.

"I wasn't going to be a Christian when I played baseball," Waits recalled, laughing about his attitude while an all-around star at Therrell High School in Atlanta. "He quickly taught me that to be a Christian, Christ has to be your life. I learned what it means to have a personal, continuous relationship with Jesus. You cannot separate Him from anything."

Waits's back-to-back no-hitters in high school attracted professional scouts. He signed with the Texas organization and after mediocre seasons in 1970-1972 in lower level minor-league ball, Waits enjoyed successful Triple-A seasons with Spokane in 1973-1974, making the All-Star team both years on his way to a combined record of 26-13.

Born May 15, 1952, in Atlanta, Waits hoped to play for Texas. But he was among three pitchers traded to Cleveland for Gaylord Perry on June 13, 1975. Called up to the major leagues five weeks later, Waits closed the season with a 6-2 record. He has been a starter for the Cleveland "Tribe" ever since.

One of many single players on the Indians, Waits is among the few who call the Bible an ally against sexual and worldly temptations.

"The road trips give you a lot of temptation, a lot of lonely hours," Waits acknowledged. "If you read the Scriptures and have a daily program of prayer and devotion, you can get closer to Christ." That enables Waits to fight temptation with Scripture, just as Jesus rebutted Satan's temptations by quoting Scriptures.

"I am human and I make mistakes," Waits added. "But I know I have a personal relationship with Christ and that He, before I start any venture, is going to help me through if I give Him full trust."

Nonbelieving teammates frequently look at Christian athletes with a judgmental eye. "They're looking at you twice as hard, looking at you to make mistakes," Waits explained. "I do make mistakes, but they know that in those mistakes I've become closer to Christ because He brought me out of them. The hardest time to live as a Christian among baseball players is when you are not following your life as a Christian, when you are slipping. That is when the players get on you."

Mostly, though, players and fans keep their reactions to themselves.

"I think Christian fans want to get to really know the Christian ballplayer better, but as a whole, I think a lot of fans believe that being a Christian will not make you as good a player because you can't be a hardnose and you can't

13

be aggressive. But that's untrue. I can be aggressive and be a Christian at the same time."

Waits and Thornton are occasional targets of cynical secular sportswriters because of their strong faith. Baseball history is full of confrontations between players and sportswriters. A Detroit pitcher, Denny McLain, once dumped a pail of water over the head of former sportswriter, Watson Spoelstra, founder and coordinator of the Baseball Chapel.

But for Waits, a player's reaction to a journalist's typewriter "only feeds wood to the fire."

"It is important not to react in a revengeful way," Waits cautioned. "I can think of a lot of players who aren't real strong in the faith. When they are attacked, they attack back. But that is the wrong procedure. You have to try to seek out the writer to talk with him alone, asking why he wrote what he did."

Jesus admonishes, "If you love only those who love you, what good is that? Even scoundrels do that much. If you are friendly only to your friends, how are you different from anyone else? Even the heathen do that" (Matt. 5:46, 47 TLB).

Waits puts it this way: "It is for us to be concerned in love, to be in prayer for such a person, not to come back against him screaming that he is wrong. We know in our hearts he is wrong but we don't need to prove it verbally. We just need to show love and concern for him."

That is the message of Jesus—love. Not just for those who love us. But for everyone, and in all situations. It can be hard. But it can be done, trusting in the Lord.

Ask Andre Thornton.

chapter two

The name "New York Yankees" is associated with some of baseball's fondest memories. Babe Ruth. Lou Gehrig. Joe DiMaggio. Mickey Mantle. Casey Stengel. Youngsters striving to play big-league baseball dream about Yankee Stadium.

A phenomenon in sports is that a winner breeds a winner. And winners attract followers. It happens with the UCLA basketball team; it happens with the Miami, Dallas, Minnesota and Oakland football teams. Youngsters yearn to play on teams with a tradition of winning. A winning history transforms the spirit of a ball club, making it extraordinary.

An almost indescribable feeling arises as soon as a visitor strides into the Yankees' locker room. So it was one particular July evening when the Yankees invaded Anaheim Stadium to challenge the Angels. That something special penetrated the atmosphere.

But Yankee ballplayers are just that—ballplayers. Most of them have an appreciation for that "special feeling of being a Yankee," but also simply appreciate the opportunity to play baseball.

One who values this chance more than most is Brian Doyle. He was as enthusiastic to share his new faith and his spiritual encounter that happened during the World Series as he was to wear the Yankee stripes.

Doyle, born January 26, 1955, in Glasgow, Kentucky, anticipated spending his 1978 summer in Tacoma, a Yankee farm club city. But injuries to Mickey Klutts and Willie Randolph resulted in Brian being summoned to the Yankees, then sent back to the minor leagues on three separate occasions. (The pattern repeated itself in 1979.)

Finally, in mid-September, Doyle was dispatched for the final time. A late season injury to Randolph, his second of the season, unexpectedly put Brian in the starting lineup for the play-offs and in the World Series. A young player who would have been content with just being on the team at World Series time was suddenly in the starting lineup.

While sportswriters scrambled to unearth material about Doyle, Brian enjoyed the type of World Series many only dream about. He batted .438, appearing in all six games. He had three hits in each of games five and six, and he collected two RBIs in the Yankees' decisive sixth game.

The box score told the story. But a tale which went unreported was Brian Doyle's spiritual encounter with Jesus as he played second base.

"During that last game, Jesus was standing beside me, and I was standing beside Him," Doyle recounted, with the excitement of a youngster opening a gift on Christmas morning. "It was an unbelievable experience. Christians will understand. It was such a deep, close experience, that it is hard to explain. But He was with me the entire game. We talked throughout it. If NBC-TV had put microphones on me, the men in white coats would have come and taken me away."

Doyle remembered telling Jesus, " 'I'm going to play for you.' I would make a play in the field, and scream, 'How do you like that, Lord?' Players from the dugout began to look at me curiously. We won the World Series, and that was a high for me, but it wasn't near the high of having that personal relationship with the Lord."

Doyle learned that his wife, Connie, experienced the same spiritual encounter as she watched her husband from the stands.

"I went back to the motel room and started to tell Connie about what happened out there," he recalled. "We both started crying. She had experienced the same relationship with our Lord at the same time. I don't know how to explain it, but I was proud that the experience happened to me. But I am also humbled that He chose me to have that relationship. If any Christian could have that relationship, he would know how much our Lord loves him."

Brian said he believes God had a purpose for his starting in the play-offs and World Series. "One of the reasons He had me there is to experience a deep, personal relationship with Jesus Christ on the field," he surmised. "I want to have that experience again because I know I was spiritually at the top of my pyramid."

Doyle's enthusiasm for the Lord sprouted during the off-season. He and his brothers were busy conducting a baseball school for 600 youngsters in Fort Lauderdale, Florida.

Brian, and his twin brothers, Blake and Denny (who is a former major leaguer with the Phillies, Angels and Red Sox), conducted the school not only to teach baseball but also to teach about faith. More than half the youngsters accepted Christ as their personal Savior.

Though raised in a Christian home, Brian said he didn't put Christ first in his life until 1977. "I felt a void in my life," he shared. "I got down on my knees and asked Jesus to come into my life and to fill that void. He is always there, steady and ready. He came into my life right that night."

The result was a new Brian Doyle. It was still the Brian Doyle who was in the middle of a five-year struggle to reach the majors, but it was a new Brian Doyle inside.

"The biggest change in my life is that I don't do anything for Brian Doyle any more," he said. "I try to do everything the way Christ would do things. It makes my life a lot easier. It gives me peace of mind. It's easier for me to live with myself. Just like they say, you become a new creature. Since the night I prayed for the Lord to enter my life, I've been a new creature."

We can all become new creatures. All we need to do is to ask, and He will make us new. Jesus says, "Ask, and you will be given what you ask for. Seek, and you will find. Knock, and the door will be opened. For everyone who asks, receives. Anyone who seeks, finds. If only you will knock the door will open" (Matt. 7:7, 8 TLB).

Doyle opened the 1979 season on the Yankee bench. But this didn't cause him to become discouraged.

"There's only one thing I can do—praise the Lord for it," Doyle said about his substitute role. "In James, it says that we are going to go through trials and tribulations and that out of these struggles we will grow in patience. There is wisdom in that. I try not to think of anything in the negative. I strongly believe that anything negative is not from God. I try to put everything in a positive perspective. I learn from my trials and tribulations."

One who writers claimed couldn't come back from his trials and tribulations was Tommy John, the Yankees' newest "fame" pitcher in 1979.

John signed as a free agent with the Yankees shortly after the 1978 World Series, ending a seven-year relationship with the Los Angeles Dodgers.

Tommy, one of the friendliest and most talkative players in baseball, has relied on his faith to overcome odds and adversity all of his life. His greatest triumph—or as John prefers, the Lord's greatest triumph for his life—came in 1976, when he made one of baseball history's greatest comebacks.

John's baseball career appeared to be over on July 17, 1974. With 13 wins to his credit, it appeared certain he would win 20. John ruptured a ligament in his left elbow in a game against the Montreal Expos. He underwent surgery two months later. Dr. Frank Jobe, in the first operation of its kind, took a tendon from John's right forearm and used it to reconstruct the southpaw's left elbow. Though the operation was a success, Jobe was among the first to predict that Tommy would never pitch again.

But Tommy John's faith in God convinced him it was the Lord's will for a miraculous comeback.

During the 1975 season, John was on the disabled list. Most baseball experts renewed their predictions that Tommy John's career was history. John, meanwhile, spent 1975 working hard. His life took on a routine which included running, exercising and physical therapy.

John returned in 1976. His 10-10 record earned him baseball's "Comeback Player of the Year" prize and the admiration of millions of fans. A year later, Tommy recorded his first 20-victory season.

"I feel that the Lord let the injury happen just to show what He could do with faith," John said in an interview, just ninety minutes before he was to take the mound.

John reported that what happened to him provides him with a more prominent platform to witness for Jesus Christ.

"After the rehabilitation, it was evident why the injury had happened," Tommy said, as he began to don his Yankee stripes. "It was a test of my strength and faith."

Christianity banks on faith. The apostle Paul says, "Now faith is the assurance of things hoped for, the conviction of things not seen. For by it the men of old received divine approval. By faith we understand that the world was created by the word of God, so that what is seen was made out of things which do not appear" (2 Heb. 11:1-3 RSV).

Though the "experts" predicted gloom, John's

faith was not hindered through the trial of what appeared to be a career-ending injury.

"Physically, the comeback was easy," he recalled. "I was going to let God do His work in my body, because there was nothing I could do. I knew the Lord was going to have to heal me. The mental aspect which accompanied the injury was hard, but because I was spiritually fit, it made it easier."

John, a gifted athlete in his home town of Terre Haute, Indiana, received thirty-five scholarship offers upon graduation from high school—all for basketball. He attended Indiana State College before the Cleveland Indians signed him in 1961. Traded to Chicago's White Sox in 1965, Tommy won 84 and lost 91 in seven seasons before his trade to the Dodgers. His seven seasons there produced an 87-42 record, with two play-off wins and a World Series mark of 1-1.

As he prepared to pitch against California, John shared more about his faith in an interview. Tommy accepted Jesus as his Savior when he was thirteen. "It was more or less an evolution process," he explained. "I was brought up in a Christian home, but made a commitment for myself after a series of classes when I was thirteen."

His Christian walk, shared with his wife, Sally, and their three children, has been nurtured by a steady diet of Scripture reading. "We try to spend as much time with Christian friends as we can," John said, as he put on his spikes. "It makes things much easier."

Another Yankee who credits his faith for making things go easier is Bucky Dent, the 1978 World Series hero. Born Russell Earl Dent in Savannah, Georgia, on November 25, 1951, Bucky was an All-State halfback at Hialeah High School in Florida, as well as a mainstay on the baseball squad.

The Chicago White Sox drafted Dent out of Miami Dade Junior College, where he earned All-American honors. He spent parts of four seasons in the minor leagues before making his major-league debut with Chicago in 1974. Ironically, it was also the first major-league baseball game he ever saw. The Yankees traded for Dent in 1977.

Dent credits his lifelong faith with helping him endure the pressures which accompany baseball.

"I think everybody is tested," he said. "But there is a purpose. I think each of us is tested every day. But if we are strong in what we believe, we'll be all right."

Teaming with Dent to give the Yankees one of baseball's best double-play combinations is Willie Randolph. He also relies on Jesus Christ for his strength.

If anyone might demand an explanation from God for a series of hardships, it is Randolph. But he hasn't. His faith has carried him through the heartbreaks of missing an All-Star game and a World Series because of injuries.

Randolph, a native of Holly Hill, South Carolina, came to the Yankees from the Pittsburgh Pirates after the 1975 season. His 1976 rookie season earned him an invitation to play in the All-Star game, but an injury put him on the bench. A hamstring injury also kept Randolph sidelined during the 1978 playoffs and World Series.

Randolph was disappointed but he was able to cope with his injuries through faith. "I believe there is a reason for everything the Lord does," he said. "He wasn't the one who hurt me."

Randolph learned at a young age in his Christian family "to put my whole being in the Lord's hands. I realize that that is why I am here. It is because of His grace. I know that if I hit .200 or strike out 10 times, or whatever, the Lord is on my side. I can always talk to Him. I always have someone to turn to. Just knowing He saved me gives me satisfaction, along with realizing that no matter how bad things may get, I still have eternity."

That makes missing a World Series seem pretty incidental.

Across town, it's another story.

The marvelous Mets—those lovable, playful men of the diamond. Those miracle kids of 1969—the team fans love to love. The team fans can accept as losers. The team that brings amusement because it isn't expected to win.

Those were the Mets of the sixties and early seventies. Those were the Mets of an era when things were fun in New York, and the Big Apple was, well, the Big Apple. But as the Big Apple turned sour, so did the patience and loyalty of New Yorkers. Fans were tolerant of a young, growing team, but the Mets of the last half of the seventies were "grown up," in the eyes of followers. So no more excuses. No more patience. No more amusement. Baseball is business, especially in New York, and winning is expected.

But for the New York Mets, winning with consistency was a habit of 1969 and the early seventies; the subsequent years have featured losing—first their all-time hurler, Tom Seaver, through a trade, and then losing ball games. Game after game after game.

Suddenly, playing for the Mets wasn't the fun it used to be. Pressure was evident. Tension developed. Patience was thin. This was the atmosphere in their New York locker room when the Mets trekked to San Francisco to play the Giants early in the 1979 season. The good-natured atmosphere of most big-league locker rooms was noticeably absent.

Even as John Stearns talked about his new faith—and how it has made him a winner regardless of what happens on the field—he was heckled by a veteran ballplayer who used foul language with a greater barrage than a steady flow of Muhammad Ali left jabs.

The intimidation seemed to be more than "good-natured" fun. It seemed like designed persecution. But John Stearns refused to let an immature veteran curb his enthusiasm to share his conversion.

Stearns, a native of Denver, Colorado, was signed out of the University of Colorado at Boulder in 1973 by the Philadelphia organization. He played minor-league ball for three years, then was traded to the Mets in the December, 1974, trade which sent popular Tug McGraw to the Phillies. John played both on the Mets and in the minors until 1977, when he cracked the Mets starting lineup.

As far as John Stearns was concerned then, his life was superb. He reached the major leagues faster than he had dreamed. His bachelor status provided him with several social opportunities. His bank account grew. He could date several different girls.

"But I wasn't really happy," Stearns recalled, responding to questions in the face of verbal abuse by a hobbling teammate. "Though I had all of these things, I was struggling," Stearns continued. "I was lonely."

During the winter of 1976 Stearns became associated with people who were Christians. "I learned that relationships are important," he said. "Christianity means relationships and treating other people like you want them to treat you. I found warmth and happiness that I never had before. I suddenly realized everything in my life had been me, me, me. I saw that instead it should be others, others, others. So I decided to accept Christ into my life and try to understand His way for living."

Learning to love others is an underlying theme of the Bible. Jesus is love. Christianity is love. Faith is loving God, believing He sent His only Son to die for our sins, and to remove us from the bondage of sin.

Stearns noted that the Bible says, "You love him even though you have never seen him; though not seeing him, you trust him; and even now you are happy with the inexpressible joy that comes from heaven itself" (1 Pet. 1:8 TLB).

Learning to love also taught John Stearns to rearrange his priorities and to reclassify what was important in his life. Baseball became secondary. Caring for people became a primary focus.

"The Christian realizes that all we have is just earthly, worldly adulation, and that it doesn't mean anything," Stearns asserted. "What really matters is our relationship with Jesus Christ, our family, our friends and others. And that's all that matters. It is hard, especially for young athletes, to realize this world is a dead-end street."

Fans tend to idolize players and to put athletes on a pedestal. Stearns believes they shouldn't. "We are just normal people," John said. "I found that out. I thought my life in baseball was going to be a fairy-tale life. I found out it isn't.

"We are just normal human beings with problems like everyone else," Stearns noted. "Just because we can go out and throw or hit a baseball doesn't make us any different than anyone else. It is important for the public to realize this. We need Jesus Christ too."

Doug Flynn, the Mets second baseman, agrees.

"It is very gratifying to know that if I have a bad day that I don't have to get mad about it," Flynn shared, as the heckler left the locker room. "I can go home, have a prayer, and thank God for giving me the strength to go out and play. A lot of people are not able to do that."

Flynn was obtained by the Mets in the trade which sent Tom Seaver to Cincinnati on June 15, 1977. Doug, a native of Lexington, Kentucky, was attending the University of Kentucky when the Reds drafted him in 1972. Playing baseball had been his lifelong ambition. His father, Robert Douglas Flynn, Sr., formerly played in the Brooklyn Dodgers' organization.

Doug's flashy fielding attracted the attention of then Cincinnati manager Sparky Anderson. Unfortunately for Flynn, the Reds had a player at second base named Joe Morgan, one of the game's best hitters and fastest runners, and steady hitter Dave Concepcion at shortstop. Flynn led the Eastern League shortstops in double plays with 97 in 1973 for Three Rivers, and led the American Association shortstops in double plays with 91 in 1974 for Indianapolis. Anderson made him a utility player for the Reds in 1975-1977, before peddling Flynn, Dan Norman, Steve Henderson and Pat Zachary to Cincinnati for Seaver.

Though raised as a Baptist, Doug credits George Foster of Cincinnati for reviving his faith.

"When I was growing up, faith was more of a ritual than a personal understanding of what a relationship with Jesus Christ meant," Flynn said.

Like Stearns, Flynn came to realize "that baseball, though important to me, wasn't the only thing in the world. After talking with other people, like George Foster, and seeing how it affects their lives, I realized I needed to get closer to the Lord."

Many of the Mets players in 1979 were struggling with their faith as well as with their baseball playing. But Doug Flynn is confident that the Baseball Chapel program is planting the seed in the hearts of several of his teammates.

"We're getting an attendance at Sunday services of between fifteen to twenty players," Doug said. "Most of the guys are searching, but this is a start. Getting them to come and listen is the first step. I know that the greater the numbers of players who accept Christ, the greater we will be able to help each other. We have a tendency to act in accordance with the people around us, so the more who accept the Lord, the better it will become."

"Just as sure as you are born, you are going to die. No matter how rich you are or how much money you have, when your time comes, all the money in the world won't save you. And you never saw a bank trust follow anyone to the graveyard."

So asserted Ralph Garr, a spunky veteran outfielder for the Chicago White Sox. Garr spoke frankly about the material aspects of baseball and faith before a White Sox game on the West Coast.

The White Sox, last winning a pennant in 1959, are like a lot of teams. There is nothing spectacular about them but there is consistent, steady .500 baseball. The eternal optimism of spring usually turns sour by summer. It's always "wait until next year."

Garr, a native of Monroe, Louisiana, is among baseball's all-time top hitters with a .309 lifetime batting average after nine seasons entering 1980. He captured the National League batting title in 1974 with a .353 average with the Atlanta Braves.

Christian athletes frequently are asked to relate their faith to their salaries. Such questioning presupposes that earning a large salary is somehow unbiblical. But that is not what the Bible proclaims. One passage admonishes, "For the love of money is the first step toward all kinds of sin" (1 Tim. 6:10 TLB). That is indeed true.

The key is understanding a player's (or anyone's) attitude toward his salary. Does the money become his god? Material success hampers spiritual growth when it keeps him from pursuing his faith in Jesus Christ.

More athletes are turning to Jesus because their material success cannot bring them the elusive happiness and peace which everyone seeks. Discovering that their money cannot buy happiness, players in baseball, and people in general, initiate a quest to latch onto something to eradicate a void in their lives. Jesus Christ fills that emptiness.

Garr, who now lives in Missouri City, Texas, with his wife, Ruby, and their three children, was raised in the South by Baptist parents. "As black people, we really didn't have much to turn to but God," he said moments before batting practice one night. "I believe in one God and that you have to turn to Him no matter who you are or how bad things are going."

For Ralph Garr, things in baseball have been mostly good. But he refuses to bask in the glory of baseball acclaim or of a commanding salary. Instead, he frequently ponders the "why" of God to keep from drifting because of his success.

"Sometimes I wonder why I am not the person who is in the hospital with braces on, or the person who was in the car crash yesterday and died. I wonder why I am not the person with cancer who is dying tomorrow. Why am I not the person who gets run over down the street? I could say why forever, but the fact remains that God is God."

Garr believes firmly that the Lord helps those who strive to help themselves. Coming from a family of ten in a poverty-stricken area of Louisiana, Garr started to help his own future by attending Grambling College, where he enjoyed a brilliant career. He led the NAIA with .568 average, prompting the Atlanta Braves to draft him in 1967.

"I didn't go around praying for God to give me this or give me that," Garr recalled. "I praised Him for the opportunity to play baseball."

And play he did! Garr quickly attained stardom in the minor leagues by winning both the batting and base-stealing titles of the Texas and International leagues in 1969 and in 1970. That earned him a promotion to the major leagues in 1971. The Braves traded Garr to the White Sox after the 1975 season, despite five good years.

A trade can shatter the security of players, especially ones who are insecure and unsure about what they will do out of baseball. Garr is unsure too. But he and other Christian players share the security of Jesus Christ. With Him and His strength, a trade is part of baseball. The future is secure.

Also obtained in a 1975 trade was Alan Bannister, a second baseman who likewise established college records. He set National Collegiate Athletic Association records for hits, RBIs and total bases at Arizona State between 1969 and 1973. The Phillies picked him to be number one in the player draft, but traded him to Chicago after brief trials as an outfielder and infielder in 1974 and 1975.

Bannister, a native of Buena Park, California, accepted Jesus as his Savior during the 1978 season after observing how faith had changed the lives of several friends and teammates.

"I think baseball tends to swell you a great

deal, especially in the big leagues," he reflected. "No matter how inflated you become or how much recognition or how many awards or how well you do, there is always a big black hole in the middle of your life. Something is still missing."

For Bannister that "something" was trust in Jesus Christ. He noted the Bible passage which says, "You can never please God without faith, without depending on him. Anyone who wants to come to God must believe that there is a God and that he rewards those who sincerely look for him" (Heb. 11:6 TLB).

Commenting on his emptiness without Christ, Bannister said, "A baseball player isn't pressed to give himself. Everything has been given to him. To give time and to give devotion and to give of yourself is a way to fill that void."

Bannister, who lives in Newport Beach with his wife, Kathleen, said his conversion modified several aspects of his life. "I don't use or abuse people the way I used to. I'm not out for me, me, me all the time. I give more of myself to other people. Baseball is something I do for a living now; it is not my whole life. That is the change I like most."

Enticements strike at anyone but Satan seems to relish making thrusts at new Christians.

"Baseball players, like other professional people, are subject to a good number of temptations," Bannister said. "On the road trips there are a lot of girls, booze, and all types of things to tempt you. We are certainly not perfect, and I still fall into old temptations. But I think I am cutting down on them. The important thing is that I am realizing them as temptations. It is almost like a rebirth in learning right from wrong all over again."

The greatest resistance to temptation comes from faith in knowing that God became man through Jesus and experienced what we experience, and that He knows our struggles. The Bible proclaims, "For since he himself has now been through suffering and temptation, he knows what it is like when we suffer and are tempted, and he is wonderfully able to help us" (Heb. 2:18 TLB).

One who helps several players with their spiritual struggles is Don Kessinger, who was the player-manager of the White Sox until his surprise resignation after half the season. Kessinger broke into the major leagues in 1965 with the Chicago Cubs. He was one of baseball's few professed Christians until the mid-1970s, when the number multiplied.

Kessinger was the first winner of the Danny Thompson Memorial Award in 1977. He was signed by the Cubs after a brilliant athletic career at the University of Mississippi, where he was named to All-Conference in baseball and basketball. He played for eleven years with the Cubs, winning two Gold Glove awards as the National League's best fielding shortstop. Kessinger was traded to the White Sox in 1977 after parts of two seasons with the St. Louis Cardinals. He was pondering his future when owner Bill Veeck surprised him with an offer to manage and play for the Sox in mid-1978.

Kessinger has observed as many changes in the personal lives of players as he has in their athletic performances. He attributes the growing number of Christians in baseball to the general born-again revolution which swept the nation in the seventies.

"Today's athletes express their feelings more openly regarding their faith and other issues than athletes did in the 1960s," Kessinger observed. "When I broke into the big leagues, the only time you heard the name of Jesus Christ in a locker room was in an improper context. But today, it is not uncommon to see a couple of players sitting around with a Bible, discussing Christian principles. Christianity today is more open. No longer do people say it is something which shouldn't be discussed, because it is a very real part of their lives. Today, as people discuss their faith openly, more come to know Jesus Christ."

Kessinger was raised in a Christian home in Forrest City, Arkansas. "Christ has always been a great part of my life," he asserted. "My faith is the most important thing to me—and my family." Kessinger lives in Memphis, Tennessee, with his wife and their two sons.

About his influence on other players, Kessinger said, "I think the greatest sermon a man can preach is the one he lives. I don't know of a great deal you can do except to live and walk your talk. That doesn't mean we don't make mistakes. We make untold numbers of mistakes every day, but yet we try our best. It is important for our actions to speak for us."

The actions of Christian teammates, coupled with the inspiration from Baseball Chapel, were instrumental in the conversion of Lamar Johnson in 1977.

Lamar, the White Sox first baseman, said, "I just had all my priorities mixed up. I knew there was something in my life that wasn't right. I was searching for it, but I didn't know what 'it' was until I kept on listening at Baseball Chapel. Then I felt that Jesus was what I needed. I needed His guidance. I accepted Him into my life, and this changed me."

Johnson noted the Bible passage which declares, "Get rid of all that is wrong in your life, both inside and outside, and humbly be glad for the wonderful message we have received, for it is able to save our souls as it takes hold of our hearts" (James 1:21 TLB).

Johnson experienced God's grace in his heart. "When I made Jesus number one in my life, every other aspect of my life became better," he said. His relationship with his wife, Valerie, was included. "My wife became a Christian too. It makes our relationship better. Our communication is better and we can rely on each other."

For a long period, Lamar Johnson relied on himself. He played minor-league baseball for seven years before the White Sox kept him on their roster in 1975. He became a starter in 1977. That season he experienced the distinction of singing "The Star-Spangled Banner" before 24,161 fans at Comiskey Park, then hitting two home runs and a double to spark the White Sox to a 2-1 win over Oakland.

But as far as Johnson is concerned, a more important distinction came the following year. He discovered the love of Jesus Christ.

chapter three

George Foster's unassuming personality is in stark contrast to many other "superstars" in professional baseball. His focus is not on himself—but on Jesus Christ. His rise to baseball stardom with the Cincinnati Reds is not a personal triumph. Foster views it as God's gift, one which grants him a greater opportunity to share his Christian faith.

Conversely, many other baseball players with impressive statistics and credentials lean on their own abilities, and give thanks only to themselves. But when the skills start to diminish for these players, or they are sidelined by injuries, self-imposed pressure mounts. But it's usually not that way for most Christian athletes. They give the pressure to God.

"There won't be any pressure if you realize things will turn out the best for those who make the best of how things turn out," Foster asserted in a clubhouse interview. The Reds' right fielder is still uncomfortable talking about himself. But not about God.

Cincinnati's famed "Big Red Machine" stalled in 1978 and entered 1979 without one of its key spark plugs—Pete Rose. Rose, among baseball's all-time top hitters with more than 3,000 career hits, played out his option in Cincinnati after sixteen years to sign a reported $800,000-per-year contract with the Philadelphia Phillies.

Like any machine, the "Big Red" needed a tuneup and some new parts. Those "new parts" in 1979 featured young pitchers Paul Moskau and Mike LaCoss, who combined for 12 wins in their first 14 decisions to give Cincinnati a quick start in the Western Division of the National League.

But an unexpected muscle pull injury to George Foster in late spring derailed the Reds, as Foster missed several games. His return sparked the Reds' surge in 1979 to overtake Houston for the National League's Western Division title. The Reds fell to the Pittsburgh Pirates for the NL crown.

Baseball hasn't always come easy for George Foster. Nor has his faith.

Raised in a strict Baptist home by his mother and sisters in Tuscaloosa, Alabama, Foster yearned at an early age to play professional sports. He signed his first professional contract at age nineteen with the San Francisco Giants' farm system. After parts of three seasons in the minor leagues, Foster earned a spot on the Giants roster in 1971. His boyhood dream had materialized.

But one month into the 1971 season, Foster was traded to Cincinnati for infielder Frank Duffy and pitcher Vern Geishert. He couldn't understand why the Giants gave up on him so quickly. Over the next eight years, Duffy hit 28 home runs and amassed a .231 batting average. Geishert failed to stay in the major leagues.

Conversely, George Foster over that span belted 170 home runs and hit for a .285 average. He won the National League's player-of-the-year honor in 1977 with 52 home runs and 149 RBIs. No other player in baseball hit more home runs from 1976 through 1978 than Foster. He smacked 121.

But for George Foster, the statistics remain statistics. He delights in his achievements. But he puts them into perspective. He refuses to point to them as the most important feature of his life. The most important aspect—his faith—had its developing roots in baseball.

After a frustrating 1973 season, the Reds sent Foster back to the minor leagues to Indianapolis, where he hit a mediocre .262 with 15 home runs. Suddenly, the realization of boyhood dreams shattered.

"I was at a crossroads then," Foster recalled.

"But it was then that I started to grow spiritually. I learned that if you get your spiritual priorities together, everything will work out. It helped me to build my mental and physical capabilities. You must have balance and you must employ all three aspects in your life—physical, mental and spiritual."

Spiritual awareness doesn't promise worldly success. Foster returned to the major leagues in 1974 to hit .264 with just 7 home runs. But it was a year of continued spiritual growth.

"My faith has enhanced every day of my life," Foster said. "I just look forward to each opportunity to grow in the Word. The better I do in baseball, the more chances I get to be a witness for Jesus Christ."

Players of Foster's stature can accumulate fortunes with off-season speaking engagements. But Foster prefers his quiet life style, sharing and living his faith. He derives satisfaction from that.

"I want to play to the best of my ability, not to gain fame, but to be able to be in the spotlight for the chance to speak to people to let them know how I feel about God. Whatever I say, hopefully, can get them on the right track."

Many baseball players pack their cards and magazines for long, lonely road trips. Foster packs his Bible. "Faith comes through hearing the Word," he asserted. "It is important to grow in order to help others. It gives me extra pleasure to know that when I go out there I am going to come through in every situation by doing the godly thing as reflected in my attitude."

Foster's boast does not carry a pledge to get a hit each time he's at bat. It promises to accept whatever happens in a Christian spirit. A hit becomes a hit. An out becomes an out. Nothing more. Nothing less.

"My action must be godly, even if I go out there and strike out four times," Foster said matter-of-factly. "I know there will be another opportunity, another situation, one in which I am able to come through and maybe win a game. But the main point is to maintain a partnership with God. Let Him be your adviser. Take His advice and keep Him first and things will work out for the best. It is just a great challenge to represent Him, not only on the baseball field, but in life."

Foster noted Jesus' loving assurance, "Don't be anxious about tomorrow. God will take care of your tomorrow too. Live one day at a time" (Matt. 6:34 TLB).

Foster also noted Jesus' assertion, "You cannot serve two masters: God and money. For you will hate one and love the other, or else the other way around" (Matt. 6:24 TLB). Foster agrees. He and other high-paid athletes are frequent targets of cynics who argue that rich jocks cannot keep a Christian life style.

"People like this believe that we should be playing for nothing," Foster said. "But the issue is not what I or anyone else makes—it is what do we do with what we make. How do we channel our money? Do we keep it for ourselves, or to help other people? Do we give to charity? I feel blessed to have a job with an opportunity to make all that money, so it is only right that I try to channel some of it back into society to try to help someone. The Bible is clear. It says to give 10 percent of what you have back to God or to the church. He is trusting us with 90 percent, so why can't we trust Him with 10 percent?"

The cynics and critics fail to understand how a Christian player rates his priorities—including his pocketbook.

"Whatever you want in life, you are going to have to give away," Foster added. "If you want love or if you want money or if you want what you have, you have to give it to receive it. By keeping it going you keep it flowing—all these blessings come back."

And blessings come in many ways. For George Foster, his baseball blessings have soared. His 52 home runs in 1977 are the third highest for a single season in National League history. His 149 RBIs that season were the most in a single campaign in 15 years. He followed with 40 homers and 120 RBIs in 1978.

But success hasn't spoiled Foster. He clings dearly to the Bible message, "Children, how hard it is for those who trust in riches to enter the Kingdom of God" (Mark 10:24 TLB). The distinction is clear: Those who trust in riches reject God. Foster, like a growing number of athletes, has riches—but he also has trust in Jesus Christ as his Savior.

There is no truer gift to share with a friend than the gracious, forgiving love of Jesus Christ. Ask Ken Griffey. His baseball career parallels that of George Foster. And thanks to Foster, so does his faith. Griffey and Foster have been on-the-road roommates since 1974.

Like many Christians, Griffey grew up in the Christian faith, but drifted. Foster's witness encouraged him to enter into a personal walk with Jesus Christ in 1976.

"I had met a lot of people who were hypocrites when I was going to church as a youngster, so I faded away from the church," Griffey said, reflecting on his childhood in Donora, Pennsylvania. "I got involved with our Lord when I got to know George."

Griffey, like Foster, is a premier hitter in baseball. After parts of six seasons in the minor leagues, Ken had his debut in 1975 with his first of three successive .300-plus seasons, followed by a respectable .288 in 1978. On a team of superstars, Griffey has been overshadowed. He doesn't hit with the power of Foster or Johnny Bench or Joe Morgan, but he handles a bat for an average as well as any of them. And he is the youngest, born April 10, 1950.

Griffey's revived faith enhanced his family relationship, especially with his two sons. "I wanted to get closer to them," he explained. "I didn't have a father, so I want to stay close to my boys."

Foster and Griffey frequently study the Bible and pray together. One who occasionally joins them is Bill Bonham, a thirty-year-old pitcher billed as a key to the Reds' comeback in 1979.

Like Foster, Bonham has tasted frustration. Off to his biggest season in 1978 with a 9-2 record at the All-Star break, Bonham incurred an elbow problem which prompted surgery to remove bone spurs. He finished the season with an 11-5 record.

The Bill Bonham who signed a contract with the Chicago Cubs in 1970 right after graduating from the University of California at Los Angeles probably wouldn't have endured the heartbreak. He would have turned bitter. But by 1978, Bonham was walking with the Lord. His faith was real. And it endured the test.

Bonham, after parts of three minor-league seasons, stuck with Chicago in 1973. After a 7-5 season, he slumped to 11-22 in 1974. In 1975, he improved to 13-15, but more importantly, he became friends with Geoffrey Zahn. Zahn, with Minnesota in 1979, was traded to the Cubs in 1975 with pitcher Eddie Solomon for Burt Hooton.

"I had made it to the big leagues, but I wasn't really happy until I met Geoff Zahn," Bonman recalled. "He was always reading the Bible and talking about it. It gave me a spark. I had always been interested, but it took seeing someone who I respected to turn that interest into faith."

Bonham committed his life to Jesus Christ that season. "It gave me more confidence in myself and in doing things day to day. When I was young, I thought that if I had a structured life with several guidelines, I wouldn't have much freedom. But I discovered when I became a Christian that Jesus' guidelines and structure give me more freedom because I can now tell what is right and what is wrong pretty quickly by listening to the Word. Before, I always judged things from the world's perspective. But the world changes; Jesus Christ doesn't."

The Holy Spirit dispenses truth. The Bible puts it like this: "When the Holy Spirit, who is truth, comes, he shall guide you into all truth, for he will not be presenting his own ideas, but will be passing on to you what he has heard. He

49

will tell you about the future" (John 16:13 TLB).

"Life changes rapidly," Bonham noted. "An atomic bomb can blow up hundreds of cities. Sexual freedom dominates people's conversation. There are a lot of things which disturb me. We need something to judge them by. We cannot just go up to someone on the street or read a newspaper to get the right answers. People don't have answers. They have to come from Jesus."

Bonham, a six-feet-three, 195-pound right-hander, relishes his job in baseball. But it has its challenges and temptations. It is not easy to travel and play games with the same twenty to thirty men for an intensified 240 days. Boredom develops. Loneliness flourishes. Patience wavers.

"I think the tempting comes for me in dealing with people with different ideas and different backgrounds, and with those who don't even like me," Bonham said. "I used to judge people by what I could see in them. But I have learned that because our Lord made everybody, I am not to judge anyone.

"I am supposed to love and accept people as they are. I have been able to create more friendships that way. I don't have to be so critical because I can accept my own shortcomings, which enables me to accept other people's shortcomings, realizing that the Lord made it that way."

A ballplayer who grasps the Lord's power and love seems better equipped to handle the temptations and disappointments in life.

Bill Bonham can attest to that.

California's Angels—the baseball ones—climbed off a bus at the Oakland Coliseum and marched toward the dressing room with the same confidence and authority that they display on a baseball diamond.

The Angels were pegged to battle Kansas City for the American League's Western Division flag in 1979 because of the acquisition of Rod Carew from Minnesota. Though Carew missed several games because of injuries, the Angels held on to win their first division title before losing the pennant to Baltimore.

The previous two springs brought the same confidence and promise—but not the results of a winner. Gene Autry, the famed cowboy who owns the Angels, had paid a bundle in the free-agent market, signing Bobby Grich from Baltimore, the late Lyman Bostock from Minnesota and Joe Rudi and Don Baylor from Oakland. Those bats, combined with the pitching of Frank Tanana and Nolan Ryan, figured to make the Angels contenders in 1977 and in 1978. Instead, they continued to lose players to injuries, and, as a result, they lost ball games.

But a new round of confidence blossomed

with Carew's arrival, combined with the resurrected bat of Grich and the rapid development of infielder Carney Lansford. Then, as in the previous two seasons, adversity struck. Carew was injured, and this forced him to miss six weeks. Tanana pitched intermittently because of arm problems. Outfielder Rick Miller was injured.

The hopes of spring looked again to be shattered before summertime. Except this time the Angels continued to win despite the injuries. A battle for the pennant would indeed materialize.

The discouragement of recurring injuries can transform a team's mental attitude. Thinking it can win, a team has a chance. Thinking it will lose, it usually does. A similar truism affects Christian players. Knowing they have faith gives them faith. When they waver about it, they can lose it.

Joe Rudi had tasted baseball victory three times before he experienced Christian victory. It makes three world championships seem insignificant in comparison.

Rudi was one of the Oakland A's who achieved national acclaim during the consecutive 1972-1974 world championship seasons. Winning championships brings satisfaction but it fails to fill a gap which can mushroom in a life without Jesus Christ. Rudi discovered this in the 1974 season.

As far as Rudi is concerned, A's manager Alvin Dark, hired in 1974, prevented him and other A's from a potential nose dive, even in the face of sports success.

While the nation was kept abreast by sportswriters about the latest contract hassles and pressures involving A's owner Charles O. Finley and most of his players, Alvin Dark worked quietly to win baseball games—and to win converts to the Lord. Dark, who had tasted the success of victory in his playing days in the 1950s, and as a manager in the 1960s, had also endured the nose dive. But when he committed his life to Jesus Christ in the sixties, it was *all* the way. Not just for off-season. He shares Christ's salvation and guidelines for living with those around him at any time.

Joe Rudi, Sal Bando and Gene Tenace are three A's who are glad he did.

"We were floating real high," Rudi recalled of the banner years. "I am thankful that Alvin came along at the time he did because I think a lot of us were heading for a big fall. You start riding high on a man's plane. But God came along at a very important time and helped us out."

Rudi, sitting in the Angel's dugout before a game against his old team, reminisced more. "Just being around Alvin and talking with him helped me. I heard from him a lot of things which I was supposed to do, things which I had pushed to the back of my mind. Alvin helped to bring them out to the forefront. My renewed faith gives me a rule or basis by which to live. I know there is more peace in my life."

Jesus brought peace which winning baseball games and being paid substantial sums of money couldn't bring. Rudi's new peace was shared with his wife, Sharon. Consequently, his life was further enriched in a manner which makes baseball secondary.

Rudi put his faith to work. He openly accepted the challenge to open his heart and to pour out the hurts. It climaxed for him and Sharon at a Christian Marriage Encounter after the 1976 season. Christian Marriage Encounter is a weekend designed to help couples make a good marriage even better. It strives to open communications between marrieds, enhancing their relationship.

"It helped Sharon and I get closer," Rudi recalled unabashedly. "It came at a great time because it was the year I went through the hassle of playing out my option in Oakland. That was a strain not only on myself but also on my family life. Marriage Encounter straightened me out. Sharon and I had been married ten years at that point but it seemed like we just met each other after that experience."

The following season further buoyed

Rudi's faith, as Baseball Chapel services featured several prominent baseball and football players, lawyers, and physicians. Their message further struck home.

"All of these people had achieved what we regard as monetary security or success," Rudi recounted. "They had everything they could possibly want—cars, houses, all the money they could spend. But they also had a real void in their lives. The more they got, the unhappier they became. The hammer finally hit and each discovered Christ as the answer to their needs."

Nolan Ryan, one of baseball's premier pitchers, discovered this truth without the leverage of a hammer. His Christian upbringing established his priorities at a young age. Fame and material success haven't altered Ryan's priorities. For him, the open ranges of Alvin, Texas, and its life style are more important than success.

A player with Ryan's credits in eleven seasons entering 1979 could easily become a year-round celebrity in the purported "money cities" of New York, Los Angeles, Boston, or Chicago. But Nolan, who began the 1979 season as the eighth all-time stikeout artist in baseball history, has other priorities, all focusing on his family and God rather than on an opportunity for off-season material gains.

"I don't think material things give the

happiness everyone is looking for," Ryan said, squatting on a bullpen bench after a workout. Between starts most pitchers follow plans designed to keep them in prime physical shape. Managers and pitching coaches eye more than a pitcher's arm. They keep tabs on his physical condition, especially pertaining to stamina.

For Nolan Ryan, Jesus Christ offers stamina. "Life is deeper than materialism. Anyone who has success for any period of time is going to realize this. They will feel there has to be something deeper. And a lot of people find that happiness comes through knowing Christ."

Raised in Refugio, Texas, Ryan grew spiritually as well as physically. "I think that as a person matures and starts to make decisions for himself, his background will have a significant influence on which way his life goes. The background which my parents gave me has had a definite impact on my life."

Fans frequently ask if Ryan gets frustrated by the occasional large number of bases on balls he yields because of his sporadic control of the ball. Can a Christian player better accept or understand the negative aspects of his game?

"Being a realistic person, I know there are going to be ups and downs and I just accept them and try to see what I can do to improve," Ryan explained. "I have peace with myself because I feel that if I try to do everything I can to have a positive outcome, then that is all I can do."

Faith also helps relief pitcher Dave LaRoche keep on an even stride. LaRoche, the club's ace reliever, was a major contributor to the Angels' second-play finish in 1978, winning 10 games and saving 25 others. He represents to relievers what Nolan Ryan represents to starters: success. LaRoche was tied with the Yankees Rich Gossage for the American League "Fireman of the Year" honor as best reliever. However, with the benefit of a playoff game against Boston, Gossage earned a save to win the 1978 award.

But not even the closeness of an important honor could discourage LaRoche. "When things go bad or represent a disappointment, I have something to believe in. And when they go good, I know there is a reason for that too."

The prestige of baseball accomplishments hasn't changed LaRoche's life style. His aim is still to grow in the Lord. Success won't change that.

"I've been a believer all of my life but now I am starting to get into my faith more," he said. "I am trying to read the Bible and other Christian literature with more consistency. I was like a blind believer before. I have learned in my reading some things about what I have believed in and why I have believed them."

The late Paul E. Little, staff evangelist with Inter-Varsity Christian Fellowship from 1950 until his death in 1975, wrote *Know Why You Believe*, a book about faith.

Little wrestles with a question asked by many of LaRoche's teammates and other players who are curious about Christianity: "Is Christianity rational?" Little puts it this way: "We don't have full answers to every question because God hasn't fully revealed His mind to us on everything. We possess enough information, however, to have solid foundation under our faith. Faith in Christianity is based on evidence. Faith in the Christian sense goes beyond reason, but not against it."

LaRoche noted, "If we have something to believe in—something as important as Christ—we can pass with the highs and lows of baseball, and not get upset. When things go bad, it is easy to blame God. In a baseball player's life, when we do bad, it is there in the newspaper for everyone to read. When we are going good, we are everyone's friend; when we are going bad, no one remembers our name."

Getting to know the Lord's name highlighted Carney Lansford's season in 1978. It was Baseball Chapel that had planted the Christian seed. His marriage after the season to a Christian woman cemented it.

Lansford was born on February 7, 1957, in

San Jose, California. He was so highly regarded by Angel management that they refused to include him in any deal for Rod Carew. Minnesota finally relented to their demand that any transaction include Lansford.

Drafted by the Angels in the third round of the 1975 summer draft, it took Lansford only two years to jump from class-AA El Paso games to a berth on the Angels' squad. His 1978 rookie season produced a .294 batting average with eight home runs and 52 RBIs, good enough for a third place finish in the American League Rookie of the Year derby. That year's award was won by Detroit's Lou Whittaker.

"From what Lansford has shown us, he is the best rookie to come up in this organization in a number of years," manager Jim Fregosi stated. "He might possibly be the best player ever developed in our system. He's got a great mental makeup for the game. He likes to play. He's an aggressive player, runs well and can steal a base."

Such a rave from a manager could make third baseman Lansford heady. But his new faith helped him to focus on God, not his abilities. "I've just started to put my playing into the hands of the Lord," he said. "I play for Him, not for myself, or for anyone else."

Lansford conceded he might not have handled his success as humbly before he became a

Christian. "I got married during the off-season and the Lord gave me a beautiful wife. He also has helped me to stay a lot calmer. Now, if I have a good game or not, it doesn't matter because I'm playing for the Lord. Things have really worked out for me since I made a commitment to Christ. Whether or not I do well is no longer the dominant aspect of my life. At least I have a chance to play. That's more than a lot of people can ask, or have asked."

Another player at peace with himself and with Christ regardless of what happens on the field is Don Baylor, the Angels' long-ball threat. A pivotal figure in the offensive arsenal, Baylor was coming off his best season with California, hitting a career high 34 home runs and 99 RBIs. Baylor, a resident of Austin, Texas, signed a six-year contract with the Angels after playing out his option in Oakland in 1976.

Fans remember Baylor for his home runs and his stolen bases—218 in five seasons with Baltimore, one with Oakland and two with California; but few know his credentials off the field. When he isn't trying to encourage the young Angels, Baylor is lending aid to another group of young people—those stricken with cystic fibrosis.

"It's a bad feeling seeing a kid with cystic fibrosis," said Baylor. "When you see a young person in that kind of shape, you realize how lucky you are." He has served as Orange County Sports Chairman for the Cystic Fibrosis Foundation. During the 1978 winter, he promoted the Don Baylor Cystic Fibrosis Golf Tournament, which netted considerable money for a worthwhile cause.

Don Baylor is an example of faith in action. He noted the message which proclaims good works. "So you see, it isn't enough just to have faith. You must also do good to prove that you have it. Faith that doesn't show itself by good works is no faith at all—it is dead and useless" (James 2:17 TLB).

"My baseball life is secondary," Baylor said, sitting in the dugout. Sweat poured from his face, the result of a vigorous pre-game workout. "Once a baseball player's career is over, you have to continue to live. Baseball is just a passing thing right now. God has helped me through a lot of things."

And Don Baylor has helped "in a lot of things" too. By faith that works.

chapter four

In baseball, as in all walks of life, there are ambitious people used by the Lord to bring others to Christ. Dave Roberts is one of the game's foremost evangelists, but he does not witness in a loud, public manner. He walks his talk. And he talks his walk. Quietly, but enthusiastically, he saves souls.

Wherever he has played, Dave Roberts has helped to change lives. He has helped players shift their attention from themselves to God. In Houston, he and several teammates, at Roberts' invitation, dropped to their knees and accepted Christ. In Detroit, Roberts used the long commute to the ballpark to share Christ. In Chicago, the tedious waiting in the bullpen was used to witness for Jesus. In San Francisco, Roberts was teamed with another leading baseball evangelist, Gary Lavelle. In Pittsburgh, he joined Manny Sanguillen.

But Roberts looks at it simply. The Lord uses

him. There is no frustration in trades. There is no frustration in a potential career-ending cut. There is no fear in the wait to see if the Lord will plant him on still another team, or even out of baseball. His future—and his faith—are placed securely in the hands of God. It removes the worry and the disappointment, which gobbles up so many players in baseball.

Early in the 1979 season, Candlestick Park became a reunion site for Dave Roberts and several former teammates on the Houston Astros. Though at the twilight of his baseball career, Dave was at the peak of his Christian walk. He exchanged pleasantries with several players, then shared, in an interview, how the Lord entered his life in 1972. So excited about his conversion, Roberts promptly shared it with longtime Astros slugger Bob Watson and pitcher Tom Griffin. Ken Forsch was revived by the new flood of faith. Those four players put spiritual life into the Astro squad, a year before Baseball Chapel launched its mission to expose players to the Lord.

Roberts' conversion is similar to the experience of many baseball players. Success didn't translate into happiness. Though he won 20 games in 1971 for San Diego, Roberts was unhappy entering the 1972 season with the Astros, following an off-season trade. Sure, the Astros were picked by writers to contend for the

National League West pennant. And yes, he did enjoy a successful season on the diamond. But the emptiness in his life gnawed relentlessly at him.

"As far as material things were concerned, I was able to buy things I thought I really wanted to make me happy," Roberts recalled. "I had security in life. The season wasn't progressing as well as in 1971, but I was pitching well. My record was decent (he ended the season at 12-7) but my earned-run average was above four runs per game and that bothered me. As the season progressed, I was like a tea kettle put on the stove in the morning; by afternoon, it is boiling and whistling. I had reached the same boiling point."

Roberts' wife had an answer.

"My wife had made a commitment to the Lord," Roberts continued. "After coming home from a frustrating road trip in August of that year, I began to wonder whether baseball should be my livelihood. My wife told me that what I needed was Jesus Christ as my Savior, and I knew she was right. We got onto our knees and we prayed together. I invited Jesus Christ into my life. He literally turned my life around. He made my marriage better. He improved my family life with the kids. He gave me happiness that material things never did—or could. I learned that only Jesus can provide happiness."

Like an excited youngster with a shiny new toy, Roberts anxiously shared his conversion with his roommate, Bob Watson. "When you find something real good you want to tell your best friend. So I told Bob. Two days later, he accepted Christ. Bob and I had some good times of sharing and fellowship. One of the most important things is to have fellowship with other Christians because this will help you keep strong. The world can pull you down real easy."

Roberts noted that the Bible admonishes that a man without Christ is controlled by his own desires and trusts in his own efforts to live life.

Another aspect of his conversion was a realization of his relationship to his family. "Among the things I continually pray for is for God to make me the spiritual leader of my household, a better husband and a better father to my kids," said Roberts. "These are the most important things in my life."

The reunion at Candlestick Park early in 1979 turned out to be the last on-field one for Roberts and Watson. Watson was traded to Boston in the American League that June. Days later, Roberts was traded to Pittsburgh.

Watson made baseball's archives in 1976 when he scored the one-millionth run in baseball history. Signed as a free agent in 1965, Watson left Houston as its all-time top batter with a career average at .299, and leading RBI-man, with 775.

Watson also recounted his conversion at the Candlestick reunion.

"Dave and I talked a lot," Watson said, describing Roberts's influence. "We basically had the same problems—our lives were out of order. So we gave our lives to Christ at the same time. I remember Dave coming over to my house. After a meal, we got down on our knees and prayed together."

Since then, Watson said, "Christ has smoothed out the peaks and valleys. My life is on a more even keel. Baseball, just like life, is a series of ups and downs. You can ride an emotional roller coaster. But over the years, I've learned how to turn it over to Him and let Him handle that. That's the thing that has helped me."

Watson also had tasted the pleasures of materialism. "At the time of my conversion, I guess I had reached a lot of my goals but I found there was a void. Since that time the Lord has been on the throne of my life. I want to say He's in control almost all the time but there are times when the old self gets back on the throne. The beautiful thing about it is that He's there, and He will always take control whenever you ask Him."

Life's temptations, though, can cause men to stumble.

"Temptations are a daily part of the game,"

Watson said. "Say a pitcher comes too close with a pitch; it is very easy for a hitter to want to go out and box his ears. And it is easy to yell and scream obscenities at the umpire and at the other team's players. There are even temptations and tests of faith associated with things that happen on your own team. For instance, in a tight game you might think that you should be hitting away but the manager has you bunting; so you call him a host of dirty names. Those are the daily things which face us."

Controlling the tongue, especially in the locker room environment of major-league baseball, is a test for every Christian player. Many who consciously attempt to avoid cursing inadvertently fall back on their "old" language.

The Bible says, "If anyone can control his tongue, it proves that he has perfect control over himself in every other way. We can make a large horse turn around and go wherever we want by means of a small bit in his mouth. And a tiny rudder makes a huge ship turn wherever the pilot wants it to go, even though the winds are strong. So also the tongue is a small thing, but what enormous damage it can do. A great forest can be set on fire by one tiny spark. And the tongue is a flame of fire. It is full of wickedness and poisons every part of the body. And the tongue is set on fire by hell itself, and can turn our whole lives into a blazing flame of destruction and disaster" (James 3:2-7 TLB).

Bob Watson and Dave Roberts didn't keep their faith a secret. They shared it.

Ken Forsch, who made baseball history in 1979 when he pitched a no-hitter, making him and his brother Bob the only brothers to hurl no-hitters, joined the Candlestick reunion. Forsch drifted from his faith in college. It took a dinner at Watson's house to bring it back.

"I still believed in God but I didn't know Jesus," Forsch recalled. "It was not really a personal commitment and at the time I didn't have much interest. But in 1972, Bob Watson, Dave Roberts and Tom Griffin and I got together at Bob's home for dinner. Bob's wife, Carol, cornered me and said, 'Ken, you have to make a decision right now.' That's when I turned things around in my life. The next day was truly an experience. I was on cloud nine and it was really something beyond description. Of course there have been downs, as happens in all conversions, but my faith is deep. He guides me."

Forsch's wife, Jonnye, truly believes in God's guidance. You can't tell her a no-hitter was simply a coincidence. She calls it "a gift from the Father." An unreported feature of the no-hitter against Atlanta was a well-placed phone call three days before the feat. Forsch's elbow was painfully swollen three days before his historic game. Doctors initially couldn't determine whether it was bursitis or an insect bite. Jonnye called the Oral Roberts prayer tower in Tulsa, Oklahoma, the next night. A caring Christian promised prayer and told the Forsches to study Isaiah 41:13: "For I, the Lord your God, hold your right hand; it is I who say to you, 'Fear not, I will help you'" (RSV). The next day, Ken's arm was relieved of pain. A day after that, he entered the record books.

Said Forsch, "I am happy with the way things have been and the way God has directed my life. As time goes on, things which I thought were going to be a detriment have turned out for my good. The most satisfying part is knowing that God takes care of me and watches out for me. That which I don't see right now will be good later on."

Anxiety about the results of endeavors can take its toll. A principle which appears evident with secure Christian ballplayers is that they have learned to release their anxiety to the Lord. But it's not always easy to avoid anxiety. Forsch can attest to that. It's not easy, for instance, if you're a pitcher knocked out of the box in the first inning.

"A lot of times you ask, 'Why?'" Ken said. "Why is this happening to me? Why are you doing this to me? It is hard and it is hard on my wife too. But I have always been able to put my faith in Him and come back to get something better. Just knowing that it is going to be all right lifts me up."

And faith also gives him a fresh perspective. "At this point, I am doing well in baseball but there have been times when I have done poorly, even to the point that I have wondered whether I should be doing something else for a living. And there are times when I thought that maybe they were going to ask me to do something else. But I always have thought that the Lord has a plan for my life. If it is not in baseball, it is going to be something else. I think that He has gotten me through a lot of tough times because I have known it is going to be all right."

Life became "all right" for Tom Griffin in the spring of 1973.

Griffin had noted the change which had dominated the lives of Watson, Roberts and his roommate, Ken Forsch, in the closing months of the 1972 season. In the following spring training, Griffin committed his life to Christ. Griffin, initially, was frightened by Roberts' witnessing.

"I didn't really understand what he was talking about," Griffin recalled. "If someone had asked me if I was a Christian I would have said, 'Yes, I go to church on Christmas and Easter and sometimes in between. I'm a pretty good guy, and I was born in America.' I thought those features made one a Christian."

But Griffin learned that a personal commitment, a surrendering of his life to Christ, was the prerequisite to being a Christian.

"I think a lot of people have the same misconception—that if they are born in America they are automatically Christians," Griffin noted. "They probably don't realize what I didn't—that there is a personal, living God. I knew there was a God and I knew there was a Christ, but I didn't know that you could have any kind of relationship until I started to talk with Dave."

Griffin accepted the Lord—and promptly had his worst spring training in the major leagues.

"But I had an inner peace like I never knew before," said Tom, who was the *Sporting News* Rookie Pitcher of the Year in 1969. "When I became a Christian, I wasn't really a rowdy guy in the first place. I didn't go out and get drunk every night and I didn't go around with women. But it made me realize that pressure is just a word. I learned that when you look at your manager or at your general manager or whoever is in authority, these people aren't the ones who are going to pass judgment on you. When you look at it on that scale, and realize that it's the Lord you're trying to please, it brings a peace which removes any degree of pressure."

After seven and one-half seasons with Houston and one and one-half with San Diego, Griffin signed with the California Angels in 1978. But he pitched very little. He was given his release after the 1978 season. At thirty, Griffin suddenly found himself without a job.

"I didn't know what I was going to do," Griffin recalled. "At that particular point I reasoned with myself that if I professed to be a Christian and if I had faith, then I was just going to have to put my trust and faith in the Lord to an all-out test. So I prayed, 'Lord, I want to play baseball.' I left it with Him."

Griffin was somewhat startled. The only team which invited him for a tryout in spring training in 1979 was the San Francisco Giants, a team that is loaded with pitching talent. The Giants have one of baseball's best crops of young pitchers.

"I prayed, 'Lord, it's up to you,' and went to spring training," Griffin said. "I went trying to make the ball club. As it turned out, I had the best spring of perhaps any pitcher except one, and I made the team. To me, that's just a great example of how much God loves His children. It means a lot to me. But I also would have praised God if He closed the doors in baseball. He means that much to me."

The development of J.R. Richard is one reason that pitchers like Roberts and Griffin ultimately were traded by the Astros. Richard's gentle voice defies his awesome appearance at six feet eight inches, 240 pounds. J.R. looks like he could play defensive end for the Houston Oilers or strong forward for the Houston Rockets. He was domineering as a prep, as indicated by his senior year at Lincoln High in Ruston, Louisiana. He didn't allow an earned run all season. In one game, he hit four consecutive home runs and drove in 10, as his team squeaked past its opponent, 48-0.

Richard's blazing fast ball brought him to the major leagues in September, 1971. He struck out 15 in his first start against San Francisco. In 1978, he became the first National League right-hander in history to strike out 300 or more batters in a single season, fanning 303. Richard shared something in common with Griffin and Roberts besides pitching. They all knew the Lord.

"I knew which road to take before I was really corrupted," J.R. said, with a wide, friendly grin. He was raised in a Baptist church and made a personal commitment to faith as a teenager. His faith brings him more happiness than, say, a 10-strikeout performance or material rewards.

"Material things are not really what you're looking for because you can run after material things for just so long before you become dissatisfied and need a new goal in life," Richard commented. "I have found that as far as a Christian is concerned, there is no new goal—there is just one thing, and it is a constant contentment in the Lord."

Images of James Rodney Richard focus on fast balls, lots of walks and strikeouts. Who would peg him as a father of five small children? Part of the American tradition in sports is to idolize the player, but not the man. We know the statistics, but not the person. We remember the reported indiscretion, but not the good deed. Today's hero is tomorrow's name from the past. The athlete seemingly is dehumanized, recognized only for sporting skills. The press can make, break or reshape an athlete's image.

"It's people who put the image on you; you don't put the image on yourself," Richard noted. "People develop their own ideas about who you are. They accept you as a ballplayer but they don't accept you as a person or accept your Christian attitude or the real person you are. They look at you and say, 'Hey, you're J.R. Richard—the ballplayer!' But I know who I really am. And I know what I really want to do."

Playing effective shortstop and witnessing for the Lord are two things which Craig Reynolds wants to do. That's why the Astros traded promising pitcher Floyd Bannister to Seattle to obtain Reynolds after the 1978 season. It was a homecoming for Craig. He was born in Houston in 1952 and attended Reagan High, where he lettered in baseball and basketball. He was the school's senior-class president and outstanding athlete in 1971. He was attending Houston Baptist University when the Pittsburgh Pirates made him their number one selection in the June, 1971, draft. After six seasons in the minors, interrupted only by brief stints with the Pirates in 1975 and 1976, Reynolds was traded to Seattle, then to the Astros.

"I'm in baseball because I think that's where God wants me to be," Reynolds shared after an infield practice. His enthusiasm was evident. "After my junior year in high school, I felt the Lord was calling me into baseball. About a year after that, I was drafted in the first round by the Pirates. That's not a coincidence. I think God has a plan for our lives. When we bring our lives to a point of unconditional submission to Him, He's going to put us where He wants us to be. I'm in baseball to give it my best for Him."

Reynolds was raised in a Christian home and taught that Christ died for his sins. "As a youngster I made a public commitment of my life and supposedly received Christ. But I hadn't. It wasn't until I was in the ninth grade that I finally looked at myself and decided I didn't have a personal faith in Jesus Christ. I had to accept Him and what He had done for my life on an individual basis. I received Him as my personal Savior."

Reynolds's faith combats the temptations associated with baseball. "We can face temptation and face trials with the attitude that Christ wants us to face them," Craig noted. "Then, of course, they can build us up in Him and in our faith."

Going hitless can be a test for baseball players. "I don't like to go 0-for-4. I wish I could get a hit, but that's the way it is. I have to accept that. I have to accept that God is working in my life. I try to do my best regardless of what has happened in past ball games. I am free in the Lord and what happens on the ball field cannot affect that."

Reynolds added, "The Christian life doesn't have to be lights around our head. Some people think that if you become a Christian, that's the end of your problems. That's not true. You are going to have problems. But the most satisfying thing is when we have these problems we can look to Him instead of to ourselves. He can solve the problems; we don't have to take them into our own hands. It is truly satisfying to know that God will handle our problems if we just give Him the chance."

Howard Hendricks, the witty and knowledgeable professor from Dallas Theological Seminary and spiritual adviser to the Dallas Cowboys, once told a sports conference:

"Tension is absolutely essential for growth, which is why God brings problems into our lives. That's why I urge Christians not to live in the past or to yearn for the future, but to live for the moment."

Craig Reynolds would agree.

In today's fickle society which demands a winner, there are still some cities in America which support a team because it is *the* team. Winning is the goal, but the team captures the hearts of fans because it represents the community. Fans suffer when the team loses, and bask in the glory of victory. Such a city is Detroit.

Though the Tigers last won a division title in 1972, attendance during the lean years from 1973-1979 totaled 9.9 million, an average of 1.4 million per season. Names like John Hiller, Steve Kemp, Jason Thompson, Jack Morris and Mark "The Bird" Fidrych are household names.

The Tigers' misfortune revolves on their placement in the strong American League Eastern Division. Despite a strong 86-76 record in 1978, Detroit finished in fifth place. The same number of wins captured the division crown for the Tigers in 1972. The 1979 season produced much of the same for Tiger faithfuls. The team was strong, but so too were division opponents.

A strong Tiger is John Hiller, the team's all-time pitcher in the number of appearances, with more than 500 in his fourteen seasons. His career has been interrupted by a near fatal heart attack in January, 1971, and a liver disorder in 1977.

Sharing his faith in a dugout interview, Hiller looked back at his banner 1973-1974 seasons which produced a major-league record of 17 relief victories in 1974. He also talked about his dismal 2-3 season which followed in 1975. Hiller said introspectively that he stumbled in both success and failure. Though baseball's premier relief pitcher for two seasons, his happiness was limited to the baseball diamond.

Dave Roberts, traded to Detroit in 1976, was a catalyst in reviving Hiller's faith. Roberts shared Christ with Hiller as the two commuted several miles each day to the ballpark.

"I think it humbles you when you finally realize you're not that important and baseball is not that important," Hiller said, focusing his eyes on pre-game batting practice. "I've learned that whether we do good or bad out on the field is not that important. In fact, I think people from all walks of life are starting to realize that our gains here on earth are nothing compared to the gains we're going to have in heaven."

Hiller, born April 9, 1943, in Scarborough, Ontario, Canada, played five years of amateur baseball in his home town. A Tiger scout liked his feisty drive, and signed him to a contract in 1963. Suddenly, John Hiller, a five-sport star in high school who liked hockey and lacrosse as much as baseball, was transplanted to Jamestown, his first minor-league stop. After portions of five seasons in the minors, Hiller arrived in the major leagues in 1968, the season Detroit won the World Series. Hiller went 9-6 that season.

Though his faith was wavering in 1971, Hiller believes today that the Lord was with him. He was felled by a serious heart attack at age twenty-seven. He missed nearly two seasons before his remarkable comeback in 1973.

But for Hiller, his *real* comeback came in 1976, when Dave Roberts helped steer his life back to Christ.

"Dave was a very stabilizing person on our club," Hiller recalled. "He was a pitcher who had had arm trouble in the past, who had some struggles on the field, and who had enjoyed success. If you could just be around him, you would appreciate how he handled his life. He always seemed to have a kind, encouraging word for somebody else no matter how big his problems were. As that season progressed, I yearned for that type of inner peace. I didn't make an immediate commitment, but through Dave and through Baseball Chapel, I learned that my life was incomplete without Christ."

His faith helped Hiller to realize that baseball isn't the most important game in the world, but a way to earn a living.

"I remember past times when I would throw a few fits if I lost," Hiller said. "Now I have an inner strength which enables me to realize that baseball is not number one, but probably way down to number five or number six on my list of life's priorities."

Hiller looked back at his youth and examined why he strayed from his Christian heritage. "I feel very strongly that if I would have had somebody that I looked up to talk about his faith that it would have kept me from straying. I grew up in a generation where a lot of people thought that Christianity and the church were not masculine. Growing up, I didn't have any big, strong athlete to associate with Christianity. So that's why it is so important for athletes today to share their faith with youngsters who look up at us. It will bring them an awareness and let them know that Jesus directs our lives."

During the off-season in 1978 Hiller addressed 2,000 adults and youth in Grand Rapids, Michigan. The experience brought more trepidation than a bases-loaded-and-no-one-out situation.

"I was very nervous because I was doing something I was not used to doing," Hiller recalled.

"Because I was a new Christian, it was even more of a challenge. But I was working for the Lord, and He wasn't going to let me mess up. I knew He would stay with me. Everything turned out fine."

Hiller hopes that his actions speak as loudly as his words. He wants people to look at him and say, "He's got himself together. He's struggling at times, but he still has himself together. He must have something I don't have and I want a part of it."

There is plenty for all in Jesus. Some people feel that God has locked them out. But they've locked God out by not opening their hearts to Christ. Hiller noted that Jesus says, "Look! I have been standing at the door and I am constantly knocking. If anyone hears me calling him and opens the door, I will come in and fellowship with him and he with me" (Rev. 3:20 TLB).

John Wockenfuss, a reserve catcher and outfielder, opened the door to his heart on May 8, 1976. He hasn't been the same since. Baseball Chapel planted the seed which grew into a commitment to Jesus Christ.

"I knew there was something missing in my life," explained Wockenfuss. The 1976 season was his first full one in the majors after seven and one-half seasons in the minors. Wockenfuss was a four-sport star in high school in Delaware.

He rejected college football and track scholarships to sign with the Washington Senators.

"All along I had put all the pressures on myself," he recalled, lifting a barbell during a clubhouse interview. "Baseball isn't as easy as it looks. I let all these pressures mount to the point where they affected my ability to play."

After receiving Jesus, Wockenfuss's outlook changed. He surrendered his pressures to the Lord.

"If I don't get a hit, I don't go home and mope about it or worry about it. That enables me to play baseball to the fullest of my ability."

His abilities make Wockenfuss a valuable utility player. After serving as backup catcher in 1976, he learned to play the outfield in 1977. His lifetime .251 average is respectable, and his ability to play several positions is an asset.

His personal life changed as dramatically as his professional conduct. "There had been times after a bad game when I would come home and be impatient with my wife and two children," Wockenfuss said. "But now I can leave the results at the ballpark."

Wockenfuss noted that a growing number of Christian athletes draw on their faith to combat the temptations which besiege professionals in the national limelight.

"There are so many temptations in baseball. There are always women around the hotels. And there is always drinking and carousing and things of this nature. But Christian athletes are better able to resist these temptations. I ask myself, 'What would Christ do?' I would fail if I didn't have God on my side."

Having pitcher Dave Tobik on his side in 1979 was not a coincidence—but an act of God, Wockenfuss believes. He has an unusual fear for a professional who is required to fly thousands of miles per season: Wockenfuss is afraid of airplane flights.

In June, 1979, a DC-10 airliner crashed in Chicago, leaving 276 people dead in the nation's worst air disaster. Two days later, Detroit was scheduled to fly from Toronto—aboard a DC-10—to play the California Angels in Anaheim. Hours before the flight, the Tigers recalled young hurler Dave Tobik from their Evansville farm team. Through a scheduling mix-up, Tobik and Wockenfuss wound up as roommates in Toronto on the eve of the flight.

"It was a trying period for me," Wockenfuss explained. "But the Lord sent Dave. We read the Psalms and we read in Peter, and it helped me. As we boarded the plane for the five-hour trip, we retrieved our Bibles and read some more. And we talked about how Jesus loves us even though we make mistakes and have fears. He loves us. That put my mind at ease."

Wockenfuss also turned to the Bible passage

in which Jesus says, "Don't be anxious about tomorrow. God will take care of your tomorrow too. Live one day at a time" (Matt. 6:34 TLB).

Tobik, raised by Christian parents in his native Cleveland, puts Jesus' admonition to practice in his life. After his graduation from Ohio University in 1975 with a degree in business administration, Tobik was the Tigers' number one draft pick. He played the last seven weeks of the 1978 season with Detroit. His impressive start at Evansville, coupled with the injuries to Detroit hurlers, prompted the Tigers to dispatch Tobik in June, 1979.

"In baseball, I know the Lord's the one who has kept me going, kept me fighting," said Tobik, moments after donning the Tiger uniform for the first time that season. "I've had my struggles over the years in the minor leagues, but He has kept me in there, persevering. He is my security—my Rock."

Helping born-again Christians mature in the Lord ranks high in Tobik's priorities. "I find satisfaction in trying to help my brothers and sisters grow and develop in the Lord."

He draws from the Bible verse, "Don't be selfish; don't live to make a good impression on others. Be humble, thinking of others as better than yourself. Don't just think about your own affairs, but be interested in others, too, and in what they are doing" (Phil. 2:3-4 TLB).

Tobik practices that directive. During the off-season, he works with juvenile delinquents. "The Lord has been leading me to spend my winter with those boys," Tobik said. "He wants me to work with them, and give of myself to them."

Don Demeter, a former major leaguer who retired in 1962, also gives himself to Christian service, teaching an adult Bible class in Oklahoma. It was there that Tiger pitcher Milt Wilcox was urged to seek compassion and help for family problems. He found much more—he found the Lord too.

Wilcox, born in Honolulu, Hawaii, on April 20, 1950, was struggling with baseball and struggling with his family in 1975. Although born in Hawaii, Wilcox played his high school baseball at Crooked Oak, Oklahoma, near Oklahoma City. He was drafted out of high school by the Cincinnati Reds.

It was like a dream. At age eighteen, he was with one of baseball's most prestigious teams. Sporting a 12-10 mark at Indianapolis in just his third minor league, Wilcox was called up by the Reds. He won 3, lost 1, and received an invitation to spring training in 1971. The glamour of professional baseball was thrilling.

The bubble burst, though, in 1971. After a 2-2 start, the Reds sent Wilcox back to the minors, then traded him to Cleveland for outfielder Ted Uhlaender. After three mediocre seasons with Cleveland, Wilcox was back in the minors, fighting tendonitis in his right pitching arm. He was also fighting himself.

"I was having some personal problems with my family," Wilcox said candidly in a bullpen interview. "I expected to be treated better by my wife than I should have expected. Once you start playing baseball, elevated to the public limelight, it is difficult to go home and to adjust to not being treated like you are in the limelight. That's what I see in retrospect now."

It is retrospective because Wilcox was willing to admit his need for help and because people like Don Demeter shared their contagious enthusiasm for Jesus Christ.

"A complete turnover came to my life," said Wilcox, who lives in Belleville, Michigan, with his wife, Lujuanda, and their two children. The following season, 1976, was another setback for Wilcox professionally. Though traded from Cleveland to Chicago, he struggled in the minors all season.

But his faith held him up.

"By then, I decided that baseball wasn't number one in my life any more," Wilcox recalled. "I used to be beside myself so much that I would go into the clubhouse after a bad performance and start throwing things. Now I realize it is a game. It is how I make my living, but it's a game. Jesus Christ is number one along with my family."

Wilcox nearly quit baseball in 1976 before his trade to the Tigers' Evansville team. Bowling strengthened his arm during the off-season, enabling him to start the 1977 season at Evansville with a 9-4 mark. Detroit called him in late June that season. He finished 6-2, then posted his career high, a 13-12 record, in 1978.

He also posted his best "people" season.

"My faith helps me relate better to other people," Wilcox said. "It's because of Jesus Christ. It's really been something—a complete turnover in my life."

Our lives can be changed by faith. The Bible puts it like this: "For God was in Christ, restoring the world to himself, no longer counting men's sins against them but blotting them out. This is the wonderful message he has given us to tell others" (2 Cor. 5:19 TLB).

Telling others can be accomplished in a variety of methods.

For Tiger teammates Mark Wagner and Lance Parrish, the Word was presented in 1976 but in contrasting ways. The result was the same, though. Each now walks with Jesus Christ.

Wagner's introduction to Christianity was unusual.

88

The Conneaut, Ohio, native, born March 4, 1954, was in seventh heaven, professionally speaking, when he was called up by the Tigers in August, 1976. Spurning a baseball and football career at Ashland College to sign with the Tigers in 1972, Mark anxiously awaited an opportunity to play in the major leagues. When he got there to replace the injured Tom Veryzer at shortstop, there was more than a glove and a bat waiting for him.

Returning from a road trip which finished in Toronto, Wagner's mail in Detroit included a *Good News for Modern Man* version of the Bible. He doesn't know who sent it. A few days later, an early fall rain delayed a game between the Tigers and Baltimore. Wagner returned to the clubhouse, kicked off his spikes, and reached for the Bible.

"I just sat there reading it," he recalled. "I had always believed in God but didn't know Him. After that, I started attending Baseball Chapel services. Now I can't learn enough about Him."

Wagner's story doesn't have a fairy-tale ending. He didn't live happily ever after in the big leagues. He opened 1977 with the Tigers, but was optioned to Evansville, where he hit .306 in sixty-four games, earning him another invitation to spring training in 1978.

Since then, Wagner has been a reserve player. But he accepts that assignment happily.

"My faith is getting stronger and stronger," he asserted. "I'd like to play every day, but right now my job is backup shortstop or second baseman, so I just try to improve on that, and with the Lord's strength, I go out there and do it."

Parrish, born June 15, 1956, in McKeesport, Pennsylvania, was the Tigers number one draft pick in 1974. He turned down a gridiron scholarship at UCLA to play baseball, and followed the path of Wagner. They were teammates in 1977 in both Evansville and Detroit. His full-rookie season in 1978 produced a .216 average with 17 home runs and a berth on *Baseball Bulletin*'s American League all-rookie team.

It also brought him closer to the Lord.

"I used to go to the bars with the guys," Parrish recalled, munching a ham sandwich after a game in Oakland. "I thought that really had a lot of meaning in my life. I still have a beer now and then, but I'm trying to keep to the Word of God."

He noted that Jesus accepts us where we are. Programs like Baseball Chapel enable many players to grow rapidly in faith. Others grow gradually. For some, the seed is planted.

Detroit's team was special. Its maturing Christians—men like Tobik, Hiller, Wockenfuss, and veteran announcer Ernie Harwell—patiently and lovingly accept colleagues at their various stages of growth, making themselves available for sharing without pushing.

An atmosphere like that allows the gradual growth and nurturing of spiritual seeds.

Jason Thompson, one of baseball's top young players, was regarded by several teammates as growing in his faith. Thompson, born in Hollywood on July 6, 1954, was Detroit's fourth draft selection in 1975 out of California State at Northridge. He played only 79 minor-league games before his major-league debut April 24, 1976.

With 17 homers and a .218 batting average, Thompson was named to the Topps Major-League Rookie All-Star Team. The next two seasons elevated Thompson to one of the most feared power hitters, as he blasted 31 homers in 1977 and 26 in 1978. The 1979 season, though, started slowly for Thompson, with only four homers by June 1.

"I think the Lord puts adversity into all of our lives," he said. "It's one of the things He gives us to build our character."

Harwell, voice of the Tigers since 1960, has seen hundreds of ballplayers come and go in Detroit. A born-again Christian as the result of a Billy Graham rally in 1961, Harwell has watched the infusion of faith into locker rooms over the 1970s, especially during the second half of the decade.

"I think what is happening is that players

today see something players didn't see before. They see that baseball is all tinsel and stardom. It is temporary, and they've got to go to something a little deeper and more meaningful."

For a growing number, that "something" is Jesus Christ. No tinsel. No stardom. But there is love.

chapter five

Standing tall in a region of America which regards lust as good and faith as abnormal is Gary Lavelle, ace relief pitcher for the San Francisco Giants. Playing and living in the San Francisco Bay Area can be a testing experience for committed Christians. It can also produce a determination not to let sordid, worldly pleasures mow down the message of Jesus Christ.

Taking the message of love and salvation to teammates is Lavelle's specialty. But like Dave Roberts, Lavelle's mission is one-on-one. "I'm not pushy," he quickly points out. He is sincere. Living his faith is a goal for Lavelle. Seven teammates credit their conversion or rededication to Lavelle's testimony and Christian life style.

The number of Christians grew so quickly on the Giants team in 1978 and 1979 that insiders facetiously waited with anticipation to see who would be next to be baptized by Lavelle in a swimming pool.

As the Giants started winning, the Bay Area started paying attention again. San Francisco fans support a winner, not a team.

Many players used the opportunity to talk not only about their batting records and careers, but about their faith. Player after player turned to praising the Lord in post-game or pre-game interviews with broadcasters. Most announcers remained silent, refusing to encourage or solicit additional information. They tried to pretend they didn't hear the players' professions of faith in the Lord.

"We have a tremendous spiritual camaraderie on this club," right fielder Jack Clark told a quiet announcer after one game early in 1979. "We have love. We praise the Lord when we're winning and losing."

"Jack, did he throw you a curve or a fast ball?" the announcer asked.

One who baffles opponents with both curves and fast balls is Lavelle. But the rise to the major leagues was tedious for him. Lavelle played in the minor leagues for eight seasons before joining the Giants at the tail end of the 1974 season. In 1975, he became more of a relief specialist.

After the season in 1975, Lavelle went to play winter ball in Venezuela. It was a trip which changed his life.

"I was searching for truth in living at that time," Lavelle recalled. "When I reached the major leagues I still had a void which needed to be filled." His hurt is all too familiar to many athletes.

Tom Johnson, then a pitcher with the Minnesota Twins, knew the answer. He had the prescription. All it took was his acknowledgment that he was a sinner, prayer for forgiveness, and a commitment to Jesus Christ as his personal Lord and Savior. The "treatments" would include daily feeding on Scripture, coupled with fellowship with other Christians and obedience to God.

Lavelle wanted that remedy!

"One night I got down on my knees and I asked the Lord to come into my life," Lavelle said. He was baptized by Johnson in a swimming pool. But the cleansing was from within.

"Because I have a personal relationship with Jesus, I feel compelled to share it," Lavelle said. "Jesus blesses us. He's with us in our good and bad moments."

Lavelle's career has experienced the range from glory to slumps. About slumps, he said, "The Lord brings me through them. The Lord said He would not test us beyond our ability to endure. I know that He will take us through our rough times as well as our good times. The ups and downs of winning and losing are tests of faith."

Returning to the Giants in 1976, Lavelle discovered that he was the only professing Christian. "Since then I have been used by Christ to share the gospel with others."

It isn't an overnight success story, by any means. Some have responded quickly to Lavelle's invitation to know Jesus; some have ignored it; and some, including his roommate, Marc Hill, have been exposed to the gospel and the Christian life style for several years before making a personal commitment.

God doesn't promise instant success. Sometimes a seed planted by a Christian today can take years to push through hardened inner soil.

But more ballplayers are coming to faith today than during any other era.

"I think mainly it is because they have discovered that the worldly things don't bring happiness," Lavelle noted, commenting on a developing truism in the story of athletes who come to faith after reaching the big leagues. "Worldly things may bring comfort to a point. But nothing, or no one, can bring happiness to a life except Christ. That's what players are searching for. That's what people in general are searching for. Let us hope they all find it."

Rob Andrews found "it." After he did, he lost his starting role in major-league baseball. But he was happier and more contented because of his faith.

"Like a lot of other guys, I had put my energies into getting into the major leagues, thinking I'd find the pot of gold at the end of the rainbow," Andrews recalled. "But I didn't find it. Society had told me I'd have all the girls, money and fame. I had those things but it wasn't making me happy."

Andrews launched his career in 1975 as starting second baseman for the Houston Astros after four minor-league seasons in the Baltimore Orioles. Rob's older brother, Mike, played with Boston, Chicago and Oakland before retiring in 1974. Traded to the Giants in 1976, Andrews started at second. But he was relegated to reserve duty when the Giants obtained Bill Madlock in 1977.

But his faith allows him joy in any role.

"I've given baseball up to the Lord," Andrews said. "I want to bring the glory to Him regardless of what I do. As I read the Bible, I see that Jesus always gave 100 percent and always gave the credit to God. The Lord blesses my performance when I do play. And He's honored my attitude. The Lord is more concerned with our attitude than with our performance."

One's attitude is closely related to one's level of obedience. The Bible says "As obedient children, do not be conformed to the passions of your former ignorance" (1 Pet. 1:14 RSV).

Raised from his "former ignorance" was Bob Knepper, an affable left-handed pitcher for the Giants who says he was an atheist just months before coming to know the Lord. He was baptized by Lavelle in a Pittsburgh swimming pool in June, 1978.

"Before I came to know the Lord, baseball was number one in my life," said Knepper, as he leaned back on a stool in the Giants' clubhouse before a game. "Now the Lord is number one. It's not important to win twenty games this year—it's important to become what the Lord wants me to become."

Knepper has become one of the National League's best left-handed pitchers. After five promising seasons in the Giants' minor leagues, Bob was called up in mid-1977, and posted an 11-9 mark. He was 16-9 in 1978.

Enthusiastic about his new faith, Knepper shared, "God wants everyone to be His disciple, but not a quiet disciple. It's our responsibility to speak out for the Lord."

Knepper said his conversion also brought strengthened love for his wife, Teri, who was a Christian. "We pray together and study the Bible together," he said.

Strong family ties buoyed by Christian faith are shared by Bill Madlock, the Giants' second baseman and former two-time National League batting champion. He was traded to Pittsburgh in June of 1979. Madlock, a native of Memphis, Tennessee, is an example of a player who developed skills after he turned professional. He was selected number 258 in the June, 1969, draft, but decided instead to attend college. After a year at Southeastern Iowa Community College, Madlock was again drafted—this time number ninety-nine. He signed with the Washington Senators' organization but soon wound up in the Cubs' system.

During his rookie season in 1974, Bill was led to the Lord by then Cubs' shortstop Don Kessinger.

"I was one of those guys who thought I was a Christian because I went to church while I was growing up," Bill recalled. "As an athlete I had money but there was something missing."

That "something" was a personal commitment to Jesus Christ. "Now the main thing is my feeling within," Bill shared. "I'm not playing for 30,000 fans. I'm playing for the 'man upstairs.' Just as you work yourself up through the minors you have to work your way up through your faith."

As "baby Christians," we need nourishment from Scripture and fellowship with other Christians. Howard Hendricks, spiritual adviser for the Dallas Cowboys football team, puts it like this: "Your spiritual growth is in direct proportion to your intake of Scriptures. How do you learn in the spiritual realm? By the same way as in the human realm—you learn by walking. And in the process of walking, we'll fall. But there is a cure. All we need do is to ask for forgiveness of sins, and renew our walk."

One who credits Lavelle with helping him renew his walk is Randy Moffitt, the Giants' right-handed relief ace. Randy is the brother of Billie Jean King, former queen of tennis. A native of Long Beach, California, he compiled an 18-10 record at Long Beach State, twice named All-California collegiate. He was tabbed as the school's most valuable player in 1969. A year later, Moffitt was signed by the Giants. After two minor-league seasons, Randy was called to the big leagues in 1972. Still he was referred to as "Billie Jean's brother."

"At the age of twenty-two, I felt that something was missing," Moffitt said. "I started talking with Lavelle and I saw how his faith had changed him. Everything seemed to be in order in his life."

Finally, in 1978, he said he "saw the light." Lavelle baptized him and his wife, Pamela, in a pool in Arizona. "My life is much more fulfilled since then," Moffitt said.

Another whose life is more fulfilled through Christianity is Mike Ivie. He explained that his conversion to Christ came about through a sports renewal conference in 1977.

"I had been straddling the fence before," said Ivie. "I learned that baseball and material things are not all there is to life. I have things in their proper perspective now. My life is not all baseball now. I went to the conference because I didn't have peace of mind. I had everything of materialistic value, but you cannot buy peace of mind."

Ivie was the first player chosen in the June, 1970, free-agent draft, tabbed by the San Diego Padres. It took him until 1975 to make the Padres, where he supplanted Willie McCovey a year later as the starting first baseman. Ironically, Ivie was traded to the Giants in 1978, and in 1979 again supplanted McCovey as a starter before the two were platooned.

Ivie, six feet four inches tall and weighing 210 pounds, discussed the temptations in professional life. "It's exceptionally tough being a Christian in professional life," he said. "You're on that road a lot and there are a lot of temptations which can lead you down the road to hell."

Focusing on the problem of temptations, the Bible says, "Happy is the man who doesn't give in and do wrong when he is tempted, for afterwards he will get as his reward the crown of life that God has promised those who love him. And remember, when someone wants to do wrong it is never God who is tempting him, for God never wants to do wrong and never tempts anyone else to do it. Temptation is the pull of man's own evil thoughts and wishes. These evil thoughts lead to evil actions and afterwards to the death penalty from God. So don't be misled, dear brothers" (James 1:12-16 TLB).

Ivie, for one, recognizes what he calls a "worldwide movement of what Christianity can do for people, and ballplayers are included. Players didn't share their faith in years past because clubs had only one or two Christians each, and they were closet-type Christians— they were outcasts—now they want to bring the glory to God."

Jack Clark, the Giants' All-Star right fielder, wants to be an active member of a team bringing glory to Jesus Christ. He credits Lavelle for his conversion. Jack caught the attention of Giant scouts in Azusa, California, in 1973, his senior year in high school. He was 11-3 as a pitcher that year, with a 1.25 ERA, and 99 strikeouts in 95 innings. He also batted .517 with five homers and 37 RBIs, as he helped place his school in the California State AA championship that year.

Promptly signed by Giant scout George Genovese, Clark hit the cover off the ball in the minor leagues at stops in Great Falls, Fresno,

Lafayette and Phoenix, with four seasons of batting averages over the .300 mark.

The Giants kept Clark on their 1977 roster, but he was platooned, much to his chagrin. His spirits dropped along with his confidence.

"I was depressed over not playing," Jack recalled in a clubhouse interview. "At times, I felt like walking out. But Gary talked with me a lot, and led me to the Lord. That took away the pressure. Now, I give God credit for my hits, wins and defeats. I give Him the defeats, which are hard to handle on your own. I credit the Lord for my twenty-seven game hitting streak in 1978. I have real peace of mind. The Bible fills me like a steak fills my physical hunger."

Now, like Lavelle, Clark says, "I almost can't get enough of telling other people about the Lord. The more I share my faith, the more the Lord blesses me. The Lord is using me as His messenger. I just want to thank Him for giving me the opportunity to play baseball."

This is true in spite of the tests and temptations of the San Francisco Bay Area.

Wayne Gross lives across and plays across the Bay from San Francisco. He knows all too well the cultural environment which drags people away from the Lord.

But he also knows the rewards of proclaiming Jesus' love.

Playing for the Oakland A's after 1976 was a test in itself. The owner traded or cut players faster than a blitz as a result of the "Orange Crush" of the Denver Broncos.

Consequently, security was nonexistent. Players knew that at the whim of management, they might be out of baseball or with a new team.

Though most found solace in the thought of a trade, others found solace through Jesus Christ. He released the tension and uncertainty in their lives. He made living for Him more fruitful than living for baseball.

Faith in the Lord eased the frustration of a sports downfall in Oakland.

The nose dive by the A's in the late seventies has been paralleled only by the Yankees during the past quarter century. After three world championship teams from 1972-1974, the A's began to fall apart, losing first Catfish Hunter through a free-agent arbitration ruling, then Reggie Jackson through a trade. Even after the glory years, Oakland won a division in 1975 and finished second in 1976.

But then, the remaining players from the championship team chose the free-agent route to escape playing for Charles O. Finley, owner of the A's. Oakland promptly dropped to sixth place in 1977 and in 1978, escaping the basement only because of the Seattle expansion team's expected inconsistency.

But those who becry the fall of the A's may forget the "great fall" of the Yankees—which was quicker than that of Oakland. After capturing the American League pennant in 1964, the Yankees dropped to sixth in 1965 and to last place in 1966.

In Oakland, an unreported factor was what happened to the lives of several key Oakland players on the 1972-1974 teams. The influence of Alvin Dark, manager of the A's in 1974 and in 1975, helped transform the lives of stars Gene Tenace, Joe Rudi and Sal Bando.

Rudi, now with California, described how he and other A's were headed for a downfall until Dark injected spiritual renewal into their lives.

Alvin Dark was fired after the 1975 season. But his accomplishments off the field carry more significance than any on-the-field achievements.

Wayne Gross, a spunky Riverside, California, native, replaced Sal Bando when Bando signed with Milwaukee before the 1977 season. Signed out of California State Polytechnic University at Pomona by the A's in 1973, Gross developed his skills in the minor leagues for four seasons. His 1976 season at Tucson featured nineteen home runs and a .324 batting average, attracting the attention of the Oakland team even before Bando's departure.

After a super rookie season during which he

hit twenty-two home runs, Gross slumped in 1978 with six home runs. Relegated to the bench to start the 1979 season, Gross was understanding. He looked for a chance to earn a starting berth—and got it when less than two weeks into the season Micky Klutts was injured.

Gross responded with a start parallel to his rookie season—hitting in the low .300s with periodic home runs and near flawless defense before slumping.

Standing around the batting cage before a game, Gross noted that baseball players have wealth, popularity and worldly possessions.

"But some of the most unhappy people in the world are baseball players," he quickly added. "Players have all the things people strive for, which is why many more are looking and finding that there is something more to life than money, fame, cars and new houses."

That "something" is a commitment to Christianity for a growing number of athletes.

Gross also noted that more players are professing faith today than in any other era. "I think a major reason for that is, as it says in the Bible, that in the last days people are going to take a stand for the Lord. The professional athlete has a tremendous platform for the Lord, and the Holy Spirit is opening up doors and people's mouths to profess the Christian faith.

"Most of the ballplayers who are playing now are in the age group who grew up during the 1960s when it seemed like everything went wrong. Really, the only thing that's solid in this whole earth is the person of Jesus Christ. People are coming to realize this, seeing that the Lord is the only answer to the unhappiness you find here on earth."

Gross noted Jesus' comment, "When the Holy Spirit, who is truth, comes, he shall guide you into all truth, for he will not be presenting his own ideas, but will be passing on to you what he has heard. He will tell you about the future" (John 16:13 TLB).

Gross, twenty-seven, takes his role as team chaplain seriously.

"The only way a Christian athlete can truly give a witness to his faith is by living it," he offered. "He can go around and say anything he wants. Actions speak louder than words."

Cynics frequently ask players how their faith stands in the face of on-the-field slumps.

"When you're in a slump I think it's easier to get back to the Lord," Gross responds. "When you're going real well, you tend to go off and do it on your own, forgetting about what got you to the big leagues, which was the talent the Lord gave you. I got into that syndrome a few times, putting Him aside and saying, 'Lord, you got me here, I'll take it the rest of the way.' But He always shows you that you've got to come back to Him."

And all players endure slumps.

"You can go 0 for 20 or make three errors in one game but the point is, how do you handle those situations?" said Gross. "There's a lot of helmet throwing and cussing, and players going crazy. If a Christian player acts that way, he's really blown his whole platform. And it is hard not to get angry. It is one of the biggest challenges I've ever been involved with. I can only get through it with the help of the Holy Spirit."

Gross noted how the Bible describes the struggle: "I love to do God's will so far as my new nature is concerned, but there is something else deep within me, in my lower nature, that is at war with my mind and wins the fight and makes me a slave to the sin that is still within me. In my mind I want to be God's willing servant but instead I find myself still enslaved to sin. So you see how it is: my new life tells me to do right, but the old nature that is still inside me loves to sin. Oh, what a terrible predicament I'm in! Who will free me from my slavery to this deadly lower nature? Thank God! It has been done by Jesus Christ our Lord. He has set me free" (Rom. 7:22-26 TLB).

That he is set free is what lifts Wayne Gross over the hurdles which accompany a 162-game schedule. Gross committed his life to Jesus Christ in 1974 when he was playing Double-A ball in Asheville, Tennessee.

"I grew up in a Christian home but it wasn't until 1974 that I really put the Lord first in my life. I had been through a lot of things at the time, things which the Lord puts us through. I wasn't doing well in baseball. My relationship with my girlfriend, who is now my wife, was deteriorating. It was a low point in my life. But I had had a Christian upbringing, so I knew where I needed to be. The Lord showed me that one night in Asheville."

Gross is open about what his faith did for his life.

"The Lord has brought my wife and me together in just an unbelievable way," he said. "It was a miracle. We had been having a lot of problems. Before our marriage, she dedicated her life to the Lord, but I was still out of relationship with Him. I knew the Lord, but I just wasn't living my faith. My wife was living for Him though. The Lord finally woke me up and my awakening brought us together. Having a Christian relationship with your wife is the way I feel that a marriage can work. You'll have your arguments, but there's a stability there that people out in the world don't have. To have a meaningful relationship in marriage in these times you have to have something besides just yourselves."

That something is Jesus. Gross draws from the Bible message which says, "Be humble and gentle. Be patient with each other, making allowances for each other's faults because of your love. Try always to be led along together by the Holy Spirit, and so be at peace with one another" (Eph. 4:2, 3 TLB).

Being at peace with one another in a locker room with twenty-five players traveling to as many as thirteen cities to play 162 games over six months can be a challenge.

But it can be achieved when a camaraderie engulfs a team, enabling players to accept the faults of others, and to praise them for what they are, rather than what they would like for them to be.

On the A's, a number of young players—many elevated to the major leagues prematurely because of the large number of veterans who played out their options in the late 1970s—are searching. As many as twenty have attended Sunday Baseball Chapel services at the ballpark.

The Grosses hold frequent Bible studies at their home during the season. "We try to keep it on a team fellowship basis," Wayne said. "We try to get everybody involved so people won't shy away from the words 'Bible study.'"

The term "Bible study" turned off A's catcher

Jim Essian until October, 1978, when he and his wife accepted the Lord.

Essian, a native of Detroit, Michigan, credits his conversion to the Baseball Chapel services on Sundays. He calls it "the beginning of our freedom and true joy and happiness in life."

"I'm still a baby Christian learning how to give up my old sinful nature and let the Lord come in and increase my spirit," Jim said.

Essian, a music and chess buff, was drafted out of Arizona State in 1970 by the Philadelphia Phillies. He played in their minor-league system for parts of five years before a trade after the 1975 season to the White Sox. After playing 79 games in 1976, Essian became the Sox starting catcher in 1977, batting .273 with 10 home runs in 114 games.

Baseball players learn not to become complacent, because today's security can be tomorrow's ticket to another club. Just as Essian figured he had won himself a regular job, Chicago unloaded him to the Oakland A's just five days before the 1978 season started.

But, in retrospect, Jim Essian is happy. He figures that even though he was traded, he found something more important than baseball: Jesus Christ.

"He has allowed me to like people and to love more," Essian said during an interview, still pounding his hand into a catcher's mitt repeatedly, almost instinctively.

The Bible describes Essian's belief like this: "Love is very patient and kind, never jealous or envious, never boastful or proud, never haughty or selfish or rude. Love does not demand its own way. It is not irritable or touchy. It does not hold grudges and will hardly even notice when others do it wrong. It is never glad about injustice, but rejoices whenever truth wins out. If you love someone you will be loyal to him no matter what the cost. You will always believe in him, always expect the best of him, and always stand your ground in defending him. All the special gifts and powers from God will someday come to an end, but love goes on forever" (1 Cor. 13:4-8 TLB).

A difficult aspect in baseball is that travel frequently removes players from Christian fellowship, unless there are active Christians on their respective teams.

"Fellowship is important, but this game with its traveling can certainly test your faith," said Essian. "The tests come in the form of drinking and going out with girls. These are real temptations. But they can be overcome with help from the Lord. It's certainly easy to find the good fellowship when you're home, but on the road, it can be difficult. There can be a lot of lonely times in hotels."

And they can be even lonelier for players without Christ.

Atlanta pitcher Adrian Devine has an appropriate name for a Christian athlete. Even if his teammates want to shrug off his message, they can't change his name.

"A few years ago a ballplayer wasn't considered a man unless he could drink so much liquor or drag so many women into motels with him," Devine said candidly in an interview on the West Coast.

"I think things have changed," he continued. "Now it takes more of a man to stand on his own two feet and speak what he believes. I believe Christian athletes should think, 'How would Jesus act in this situation?' If we ask that before we act, our actions will be guided."

Devine's team, the Atlanta Braves, is a club with a changing heritage; three homes in 104 years have marked the Braves, first organized in Boston in 1876 before moving to Milwaukee in 1953 for a 13-year stretch, which included champion teams in 1957-1958.

But since moving to Atlanta in 1965, winning has become a memory, not a reality. Except for winning the National League Eastern Division pennant in 1969, but losing to the Mets to determine the World Series representative, the Braves have failed to finish above third place. The 1976-1979 teams have all finished in last place.

Playing on a losing team can be discouraging.

But playing for the Lord puts wins and losses into a different perspective—the goal to win still remains, but a Christian athlete is better equipped to handle defeat.

Handling defeat or victory is a privilege for Devine, who is six-feet-four-inches tall, a native of Galveston, Texas. Plagued by injuries throughout his career, Adrian believes God's grace has brought him back each time. Devine was drafted by the Braves as a freshman at Sam Houston State University.

In his second major-league season, Devine experienced severe pain in his right elbow. He discovered, through his wife-to-be, Gloria, that he had pains elsewhere too. Spiritual ones.

"She helped me realize that I had only been going through the motions," Devine recalled. "Gloria told me it was about time I became sincere about my faith. I made a simple commitment; I stated that I wanted Christ to come into my life and change it. I acknowledged my sins and my needs. And that time, I was doing some things in life I knew I shouldn't have been doing. From that point on, I have turned these things over to God and have tried to live my life the way He wants me to live it. I remain prayerful about what He wants me to do in baseball as well as out of it."

Devine pointed to Jesus' advice on prayer, "Keep on asking and you will keep on getting; keep on looking and you will keep on finding;

knock and the door will be opened. Everyone who asks, receives; all who seek, find; and the door is opened to everyone who knocks" (Luke 11:9, 10 TLB).

Devine won 12 and lost 8 with Savannah in 1972, but was plagued with recurring shoulder problems in 1973 and 1974, curbing his effectiveness. But his faith held steadfast.

"In 1974, I went to four different doctors in four different states and they told me to give up baseball and to never pitch again," Devine recalled. "I kept praying about it. During that off-season I taught a teen-age Bible class, and left my future in baseball to the Lord. I prayed, 'Lord, if you want me to play baseball, you've got to heal the arm. If you don't want me to play, let me know what you want me to do.'"

He went to spring training in 1975 expecting to be released.

"But the pain in my shoulder disappeared. I gradually started throwing the ball real well. I made it to the major leagues in the fall of 1975, and I've been here ever since. I'm positive it is because God wants me here."

Devine said that his profession provides him opportunities to minister to youngsters and adults at several churches. During one off-season he was a missionary in Japan. Devine's activities focus on the admonition of the apostle James, "So you see, it isn't enough just to have faith. You must also do good to prove that you have it. Faith that doesn't show itself by good works is no faith at all—it is dead and useless" (James 2:17 TLB).

An ability to relax accompanies Devine's faith. "It's really interesting that a lot of people these days are dying of heart attacks at a younger age because life is just too fast for them," he noted. "They just can't sit back and relax. I'm thankful I have the attitude that no matter what happens I shouldn't be so worried that I disturb people around me, including my family. I know that I'm loved by God and that He will take care of me."

Devine was born on December 2, 1951. He makes $100,000 per year in baseball. He has seen what the material aspects of baseball can do to players.

"You have to be very careful with the money aspect of the game," he said. "I have things now that I never dreamed of owning. I always thought that if I earned $50,000 it would put me on the top of the world. I'm earning double that but I've discovered that money doesn't buy happiness. I'm so thankful for my health and my family."

Many ballplayers frequently worry about tax investments because their large salaries boost them into high tax brackets.

"Players often bring more worries on themselves by worrying about their investments," Devine said. "The way I see it, though, is that I shouldn't have any worries at all. Christ has promised me eternal life. There is just a short time here on earth, so why in the world should I worry about things like clothing, housing and material luxuries? That doesn't mean I can just sit back and do nothing. I am concerned about my career and my talents. But I have seen too many athletes get tied up with the money aspect, playing with drugs, liquor and women. When I first signed, I was the same way. But, fortunately, I found out that these things don't bring happiness. Jesus brings happiness."

To help teammates, Devine describes how Christ died once and for all to end sin's power and how He lives forever in an unbroken relationship with God.

"Your old evil desires were nailed to the cross with him," Paul says, "that part of you that loves to sin was crushed and fatally wounded, so that your sin-loving body is no longer under sin's control, no longer needs to be a slave to sin" (Rom. 6:6 TLB).

Buddy Solomon, another pitcher for the Braves, said his sinful nature once made him a bitter person. Like teammate Glenn Hubbard, Solomon frequently saw evil in others. Hubbard, a young second baseman, asserted that before he came to know the Lord in 1977, his life style was negative and violent.

"I'd do anything to win," said Hubbard, relishing in the day-after glory of a three-run homer to beat the San Francisco Giants. "I used to go out there and try to hurt the other guy, to put him out of the game. I would try to hurt the pitcher by hitting the ball at him. I'd do anything to win."

Solomon's actions were less physical, but just as emotional. Bitterness swelled in both Hubbard and Solomon. But in different ways at different times, Jesus Christ delivered them from their bitterness. The Bible says, "For whatever God says to us is full of living power; it is sharper than the sharpest dagger, cutting swift and deep into our innermost thoughts and desires with all their parts, exposing us for what we really are. He knows about everyone, everywhere. Everything about us is bare and wide open to the all-seeing eyes of our living God; nothing can be hidden from him to whom we must explain all that we have done" (Heb. 4:12, 13 TLB).

Exposure to Baseball Chapel services gradually brought Hubbard to faith.

Born on September 25, 1957, at Hann Air Force Base in Germany, Hubbard was drafted out of high school in Ogden, Utah, and flourished in the minor leagues until July, 1978, when the Braves called him up.

"My faith has helped me to relax—and to control my temper," Hubbard said calmly.

Solomon drifted from his childhood faith when he entered professional baseball in 1969 after his draft by the Dodgers. He has played with four teams. Baseball Chapel services "helped me to see that it was best for Buddy to get back on the right track."

The results:

"I'm a better person with inner peace," Solomon asserted. "My faith makes a difference in my personality. It makes me the person I was brought up to be. I'm glad to be on the right track."

The Bible describes it this way: "Don't worry about anything; instead, pray about everything; tell God your needs and don't forget to thank him for his answers. If you do this you will experience God's peace, which is far more wonderful than the human mind can understand. His peace will keep your thoughts and your hearts quiet and at rest as you trust in Christ Jesus" (Phil. 4:6, 7 TLB).

That makes playing on a last-place team bearable.

chapter six

Jerry Terrell's name carries an impact in baseball. It's associated with his nicknames: Preacher, Sanctified, Reverend, Holy of Holies, and 10:9.

He may be the game's only player who ever chose his team based on where he thought the Lord could use him—not to swing a bat, but to share Jesus Christ.

Terrell is a utility player for the Kansas City Royals. But he's in the starting lineup for God every day, living his faith with bubbling enthusiasm.

In the midst of deep disappointment among Royal players because of the heartbreaks of losing to the Yankees for three consecutive years in the playoffs, Terrell symbolizes hope. He leaves the results in the locker room. Each tomorrow is a new day, a new start for him. Happiness comes from knowing the Lord, not winning baseball games. Winning is important to Jerry, but a Christian attitude is more so. So walks Jerry Terrell.

After five years in Minnesota, including two as a teammate of the late Danny Thompson, Terrell played out his option. How could a Christian play out his option?

"When I was negotiating my contract in 1977, God made it very clear to me that He didn't want me in Minnesota," Terrell said in an interview. "The contract that was offered me was a multi-year one with a 20 percent cut the first year, an 18 percent cut the next year and a 5 percent cut the third year. I saw that after the first year I'd be making less than the minimum wage in baseball. That made it quite obvious that I wasn't supposed to be there."

The free-agent reentry draft, at that time, consisted primarily of what Terrell laughingly refers to as the "brand names"—the Jacksons, the Zisks, the Johns, the Torrezes, the Forresters, the Baylors, the Rudis, the Bandos, the Hisles. Would a club want a utility player named Terrell?

In the event he would be drafted, Terrell hired an agent to represent him across the nation. The negotiator, though, had a suggestion for him: "If you want to stay in baseball, you'd better accept the Minnesota offer, or you'll be pumping gas."

Terrell recalled, again with a chuckle, "I told

him if I'm going to be pumping gas, that's great if it is what the Lord wants me to do. There were two different attitudes at that point. I had peace and contentment. The negotiator was utterly frustrated, unable to believe my position. He came back with, 'Well, God helps those who help themselves—it's in the Bible.' And I said, 'That, sir, is not in the Bible. It's a quotation from Benjamin Franklin.'"

While the negotiator paced, Terrell prayed.

"I didn't know if I was supposed to be in baseball or what," he remembered. "I viewed it as a type of trial which God takes you through. I thought of 1 Corinthians 10:13, and figured God would provide the answer. I knew it was a test."

This particular Bible passage asserts, "But remember this—the wrong desires that come into your life aren't anything new and different. Many others have faced exactly the same problems before you. And no temptation is irresistible. You can trust God to keep the temptation from becoming so strong that you can't stand up against it, for he has promised this and will do what he says. He will show you how to escape temptation's power so that you can bear up patiently against it" (1 Cor. 10:13 TLB).

The 1977 season ended, and Terrell's patience endured. He didn't even look for a job. He and his wife prayed continually.

123

Then, in December, the phone rang. It was the agent. "Jerry," he began, "you're not going to believe this! Nine teams drafted you."

Terrell described his feelings his way, "My wife and I were very happy. We saw that God made it clear He wanted us in baseball. The question now was—where?"

That's easy—whoever bids the highest, right? Wrong.

Terrell prayed for the Lord to lead him to the team which could most use his Christian witness.

"San Francisco was one of the first teams to draft me and I like San Francisco," Terrell recalled. "But they had a solid core of Christians on their team and I didn't feel that was where the Lord wanted me."

Kansas City, here he comes.

Terrell came to spring training with the Royals to start the 1978 season. Evident was the lingering disappointment of the two previous falls. Twice, Kansas City had the Yankees on the rope and an excellent shot at winning the American League crown. But each time, New York rallied to win. The disappointment tended to breed pressure.

For Jerry Terrell, the Lord's opportunity would present a challenge. Though many Royals attended Baseball Chapel, few were professing, practicing Christians.

Terrell's attitude startled his new teammates.

"I told them that God looks at it this way: He could care less whether Kansas City won or lost the playoffs. What made a winner in His eyes was one's attitude. Did the team give 100 percent? Then that pleases God."

What Terrell saw was that "winning and losing were everything to them for the simple reason that they can't see beyond that aspect. It's really a tough letdown on the guys to lose in the playoffs like that. It's just one of those things; it's a worldly attitude."

The pressure to win, coupled with the material rewards of successful seasons, blocked several teammates from the Christian message.

"A problem with many players is that they're afraid that if they give their life to Jesus He's going to take everything away from them," Terrell said. "That's not true. Just because you're a Christian doesn't mean you're going to Africa to be a missionary."

Relating that to nonbelieving teammates, though, was difficult—initially.

"I'd try to explain to them that once you give your life to Christ completely, yes, He may take it away but more than likely He won't. The object is that when you give your life to Christ you've got to be *willing* to give up everything you have. You'll probably get more than you ever dreamed about back, but you still have to be willing to give it to Him. I'm still working on trying to describe that to the guys."

After a steady 1978 season on the field, Terrell returned for the 1979 season with renewed eagerness. But he was an early-season injury casualty, missing 36 games. When he returned, he still played very little on the talent-laden Royals. But his work for the Lord with the Royals multiplied. Terrell launched a Bible study. He marveled, "On the Minnesota team, we had a core of believers but we never had a Bible study. Here we have one with a group of nonbelievers."

At the same time, Terrell's wife launched a Bible study in Kansas City for the players' wives.

"We're planting seeds," Terrell quipped. "We have some players and wives who have the possibility of becoming Christians. The way I look at it is that after we get a foundation started here, I'll be gone. Where, I don't know, but I'll be gone. The Lord will have another opportunity for me elsewhere."

The material rewards of baseball distract many nonbelievers from the Lord.

"The more materialistic you get, the more money you have and the more you want," Terrell said. "The Lord has dealt with me in that area. When I negotiated my contract I had higher offers from other clubs, more than what Kansas City offered me, but I really believe God

126

will allow you to have what you can handle and not more than that. If someone has more than he can handle, he takes his eyes off the Lord and puts it on the materialistic things.

"The players with large salaries are seeing money, big houses, fancy cars, and lots of fun things. They're channeling their time towards those areas, putting the Lord over in a closet. Their focus is on baseball, how to earn more money and how to get more things. It may be temporary pleasure, but that's what sin is—temporary pleasure. I'll be the first to admit that there is fun in sin, but it's only temporary. I try to relate that to my teammates."

Terrell's strong stand for the Lord has produced a host of nicknames, including 10:9, a play on words over Terrell's practice of signing Romans 10:9 with his autograph.

The passage asserts, "For if you tell others with your own mouth that Jesus Christ is your Lord, and believe in your own heart that God has raised him from the dead, you will be saved" (TLB).

Terrell sees growth in such good-natured ribbing.

"I'll take the brunt of the attack if it gets them thinking about it because in order to get on my case they've got to at least be thinking about it."

Terrell's faith hasn't always been strong. He remembers when he broke into the major leagues in 1973.

"I would root for my teammates outwardly, but inwardly I was hoping maybe one of them would sprain an ankle so maybe I could get out there, show them I was a superstar and make the big bucks. God eventually taught me that my perspective was wrong. It involved chasing after materialistic, worldly things. Now when I root for my teammates, I'm rooting for them because that's the way God would want me to do."

Terrell, a native of Waseca, Minnesota, made a public profession of faith at a Bible camp when he was twelve.

"Counselors explained to me about God's love and how He sent His Son, Jesus Christ, to die for my sins," Terrell recalled. "I thought, 'Well, I'm a Christian now.' But the problem was that I had it from the neck up, and that's where it stayed. I even had all the Christian terms, my own testimony, and everything. But the problem was that I went through life without that assurance in my heart. It really bugged me because doubt kept flashing in my mind when people would ask, 'Do you know where you're going when you die?' I'd say, 'Sure, I'm going to heaven.' But I really wasn't sure because I didn't know if I had Jesus in my heart."

During an off-season, Terrell attended a Bible study on the Book of Acts at a church in Sun Valley, California.

"The point was made that once you ask Jesus Christ into your heart you never have to do so again and to continue to do so was to insult God," Terrell said. "The problem I had was that I didn't know for sure whether or not I had asked Jesus Christ into my heart, but I didn't want to insult God. So it really frustrated me. I didn't know what to do. One day I went to a friend at church and said, 'Lou, I'm in trouble. I don't know if I'm a Christian or not.' He said, 'What do you mean? You talk like a Christian and you act like a Christian.' "

But there is a difference, Terrell noted. The key lies with the heart.

"I told Lou, 'I don't know if I've made a heartfelt commitment. I don't want to insult God.' He smiled and put his arm around me and said, 'Jerry, I'll tell you something. God loves you unconditionally. He loves you just the way you are and He doesn't want any doubt in your mind. You're not going to insult the Creator of the universe by asking Christ into your heart right now.' "

So on February 9, 1975, away from the cheers and jeers which dominate an athlete's life, Jerry Terrell dropped to his knees in a room at a church in Sun Valley, California.

"I prayed, 'Lord, just in case I didn't ask, I want you in my heart. I'm not perfect and I know you are the only perfect One who ever walked this earth and I just thank you for the pain and suffering you went through for me. Even more so I want to thank you for coming back from the dead. I claim your victory over death for my own and I want you to be in my heart and be my Lord and Savior forever.' "

There was no lightning, and it was not an emotional experience. But there was an assurance in Jerry Terrell's heart, a certain peace which no one can take away.

"There's no more doubt in my mind," Terrell said. "I know Jesus Christ is in my heart. I didn't give Him 99.99 percent, I gave him 100 percent of my life to do with as He wants. I'm trying to live in the manner suggested by the verse in 1 Corinthians 10:31."

That passage says, "You must do everything for the glory of God, even your eating and drinking" (TLB).

"That's my purpose as a Christian—whether I'm playing baseball, sitting on the bench or walking across the street. My purpose is to glorify God."

Danny Thompson was one baseball player who glorified the Lord. Dying from leukemia, he played ball until just prior to his death in 1976, and was an inspiration to many. Terrell and Thompson were teammates in Minnesota in 1973 and in 1974, before Thompson's trade to Texas. Terrell was one of twelve nominees in

1979 for the third annual Thompson award, bestowed annually on the player who best exemplifies the Christian spirit in his life.

The public disclosure of Thompson's illness attracted several unsolicited "cures."

"Everyone knew how he could be healed," Terrell recalled. "He heard every suggestion, from putting his hand on a bunch of medallions to going to a doctor in Mexico. He saw all the possible avenues, all the ways to go, but picked the correct one. He told me in the fall of the 1974 season, 'Jerry, I see all the ways to go but the one true way is with the Lord.'"

Terrell, moved by emotion, further recalled Thompson, asserting, "You couldn't have met a finer gentleman. If there was any way of earning your way to heaven, he was one of the guys who could have done it. But, of course, that's not possible, so you need that one-on-one relationship with Christ. Danny steered his good works toward helping other people come to know the Lord. He really had an impact on my life."

Now, old 10:9 is trying to have an impact on lives too—his teammates'.

Down the freeway two hundred miles, the artistic arches of St. Louis pierce skyward. In the horizon is Cardinal Stadium, a massive piece of concrete architecture which blends with the downtown theme of expansive buildings. St. Louis is another "sports town" which loves its team whether it's winning or losing.

In the state of Missouri, winning has been a Kansas City tradition in the 1970s. The Cardinals last captured a National League crown in 1968, but lost to Detroit in the World Series.

A winner on the field during the 1970s was Ted Simmons, the Cardinals' talented catcher-third baseman. Simmons closed the 1970s with a lifetime average of .302.

He is another gifted athlete who could have picked his sports. Simmons turned down football scholarship offers from Ohio State, Michigan, Michigan State, Purdue and Colorado to play professional baseball.

In a private, quiet way, Simmons is a leader. He isn't vocal like many of baseball's "superstars." At times, he even appears annoyed. But Simmons lets his bat talk for him.

Simmons was baptized at age fourteen. He refused to let the temptations and enticements of his teen-age years distract him from Jesus Christ.

"The thing that's kept me in my faith are all the countless situations in my life that most people would write off as coincidences that I have not been able to write off as coincidences," Simmons said in an interview. "My prayers were answered time and again in my life. . . . I suppose I could share a hundred of them but I think the things that have happened are between myself and Christ. They are situations that are very personal to me and I think my experiences are comparable to what other Christians have experienced. I don't think a purpose is served by opening up about a one-on-one relationship with God to the masses of people. And unfortunately, the masses aren't interested anyway."

Simmons, who finished second in batting in the National League in 1975 with a career high .332 average, commented that many people ignore the Christian message. "People won't listen to what you say," Simmons said. "I think Christ's life was the best example of that. The only reason Christ is remembered today is because He lived His life a certain way. Sure, people took what He said and forever have been trying to interpret it. But there is one thing people cannot argue about, and that's the way Christ lived His life. I think that is the one thing that all Christians have to keep in mind: People don't listen to what you say. Christ is the best example of that. People only listen or pay attention to what you do and the way you live your life. That's the best witness for anybody, from a baseball player to an accountant to a gas station attendant."

Buddy Schultz tries to live his faith. It means

surrendering control to Jesus, and allowing Him to guide your life. It might mean victories. It might mean defeats. It definitely means salvation, peace and happiness.

Schultz, a relief pitcher, played minor-league ball for parts of four seasons before the Chicago Cubs called him up in 1975. He played for the Cubs for only parts of two seasons, but long enough to be inspired by Don Kessinger, the longtime Cub shortstop who ironically came to St. Louis, as did Schultz, in a 1977 transaction.

"I had always wanted absolute proof about believing in Jesus," Schultz recalled. "I wanted to have all the answers. I had to have proof for everything."

Slowly, but progressively, Baseball Chapel services hammered at Schultz's heart.

"I came to realize that it's a faith—a faith based on strong evidence," Schultz asserted. "I asked Jesus Christ to come into my life. It's hard because sometimes you don't understand what that means. I know that I feel 100 percent better than I did before. And I know the impact He's had on my emotions, my pressures and my family relations."

Family relations can be strained for professional athletes. But with God, there is a confidence and trust which ease the loneliness that comes from long departures.

Thousands of fans on any particular day jam stadiums to root for their teams. But behind the public display of glamour and prestige lies an abundance of loneliness in the lives of players. Playing major-league baseball is fun, and frequently exciting. But the long stretches away from home can be terribly agonizing. Most players are young men with young families. The wives and children are the unsung heroes of sports. They are the ones who alter their life styles to accommodate part-time fathers and husbands.

Buddy Schultz is painfully aware of these separations and their impact on his family.

"It's extremely hard, especially on the children," he reflected.

Schultz, like most players, tries to keep his children in one city so that their education will not be interrupted by constant transfers from one city to another. Consequently, separations can be aggravated, particularly if a player doesn't live in the city in which he plays.

God and the telephone serve as a player's allies against loneliness. Schultz and many other players turn to the Lord in their despair, relinquishing the hurts and anticipation.

"During the off-season, I try not to work, or if I do, I try to make it marginal so that I can spend as much time as possible with my family during those five months," Schultz asserted.

135

A starting pitcher who Schultz frequently relieved is John Denny, a six-feet-three native of Skull Valley, Arizona. Like Schultz, Denny's faith has prospered as a result of Baseball Chapel services.

Finding Jesus Christ helped Denny find himself.

"It has helped me mature as a person," the Cardinal right-hander asserted. Denny said chapel services had brought out his dormant faith.

"Before, I might have been a little shy, timid and embarrassed to talk about my faith in the open," he said. "I'm not now, and that's been a big advance for me. I just want to continue to grow."

Denny's shyness stemmed from his background. He went from a ranch outside of Prescott, Arizona, to minor-league baseball in 1970. Learning to pitch and to communicate dovetailed together for him.

After portions of six seasons in the minors, Denny climbed to the major leagues in 1975. He fashioned a 10-7 record, followed by 11-9, 8-8, and 14-11. Coming into 1979, Denny had never experienced a losing season.

But 1979 started inauspiciously. By mid-season, Denny was 3-6 with an earned-run average of 4.80. Also mired in a slump was Bob Forsch, another key starter.

A slump is inevitable in baseball. Coming to that realization keeps Denny from utter despair.

"Since my faith has grown, especially in the last couple of years, I can deal with a slump much more maturely than before," Denny said. "A few years ago I probably would have receded into a shell and have been worried about what was going on in the profession. I would have felt like the world was ending. But the Lord has shown me that the world still turns and that there are other ways to accept your failures by the presence of things around you. It makes it easier. My faith helps me to keep trying."

Forsch's faith is his ally too. The six-feet-four, 200-pound right-hander is the older brother of Ken Forsch, the hurler with Houston.

Bob is an example of faith. He was selected in the thirty-eighth round by the St. Louis Cardinals in 1968, a precarious draft position for a would-be professional baseball player. But Forsch put faith in his abilities and in the Lord. After four and one half minor-league seasons, he climbed to the Cardinals in 1974. His lifetime record was 62-47 entering 1979, including a 20-game season in 1977.

"Baseball is an up-and-down game, and when you believe in Jesus Christ, I think it makes life easier when things aren't going well," Forsch said. "And when things are going well, I have someone to thank."

Forsch doesn't fret about a slump. "I look for the good in it, not the bad. I look at it positively. He's given me so much. He has allowed me to be in the big leagues, make a good salary, and have a fine home. I don't think a Christian should look on the negative side. I think the idea is to be thankful for what you have."

Another positive believer is Mark Littell, who combines with Schultz to give St. Louis a highly touted relief corps.

Littell, a native of Cape Girardeau, Missouri, has enjoyed his professional career in his home state. He pitched for Kansas City for two full seasons and portions of two others before being traded to St. Louis after the 1977 season.

Littell's faith matured after the 1973 season. It was then, he said, that he discovered he had been taking God for granted. He had finished a 16-6 season at Omaha in Triple-A ball and 1-3 for the Royals.

"I had a great year and I should have thanked God," Littell recalled. "I was twenty years old and really on top of the world."

An arm injury brought Littell's focus back to the Lord.

"I asked God to forgive me for taking Him for granted all along," Littell said. "I asked Him to lead me in baseball or wherever. I pledged to do it His way and not by myself any more. When that happened, I started growing. I hope I never stop growing in that respect."

Littell's arm healed and he went 16-15 at Omaha the next one and one half seasons before being called up to the major leagues to stay. An added benefit was Baseball Chapel services, which at that point in 1975 hadn't been inaugurated in the minor leagues.

"Baseball Chapel is probably the best thing that ever happened in athletics," Littell asserted.

There are lives throughout the major leagues that attest to that. Changed lives.

Tom Paciorek of the Seattle Mariners is a prime example of a changed life. He has ridden the athletic roller coaster from the minor leagues' player of the year to sudden unemployment. He has played for the best and for the worst. He has played well and he has slumped miserably.

Now, playing in Seattle, it was a privilege. The Mariners, only in their third year in 1979, represented to many in baseball a dead-end road for an ambitious baseball player. Expansion teams generally lose for several seasons and the frustration can become dominating. A player for a losing team can become a loser. Ones who escape that stigma regardless of the results are Christians who give their wins and losses to the Lord.

Paciorek, an affable, good-looking man, starred in football and baseball at the University of Houston after an outstanding prep career in Detroit. At Houston, Paciorek earned All-American honors in baseball during his junior and senior years. He also earned honorable mention as an All-America defensive back on the Cougars' flashy football team. Paciorek was drafted by the Miami Dolphins in football and by the Los Angeles Dodgers in baseball. He chose baseball.

Paciorek's minor-league career included the esteem of being selected Player of the Year in 1971 by the prestigious *The Sporting News*. Tom's career looked bright.

But after five full seasons, three with Los Angeles and two with Atlanta, Paciorek's baseball world crumbled. He's glad it did. After the 1978 season, Atlanta handed Tom his unconditional release. He found himself playing minor-league baseball in San Jose, California.

This humiliation and experience could have broken Tom Paciorek. Similar situations have destroyed many athletes. But instead, Paciorek was reborn. Just as Jesus told Nicodemus that to see the glory of salvation he must be born again in Christ, Tom Paciorek marveled in the spiritual awakening.

"I felt that my release by Atlanta was unjustified at the time," Paciorek said, freely discussing his conversion in the Mariners' locker room. "I felt bitter toward most things in general after the release. I was without a job for the first time in twelve years."

His conversion, Paciorek laughed, may be the first attributed to a Toyota car.

"I came to know the Lord at that time completely by chance," he began. "The easiest way to explain it is that I had tried just about every way to live my life. Well, like that Toyota car commercial, I said, 'Okay, God, what have you got to offer me now?'"

Like for most Christians, it was an offer he couldn't refuse.

"I know it's not the greatest way to come to know the Lord, but that's just the way it happened," Paciorek said.

Now, he is an enthusiastic ambassador for Jesus Christ.

"In times when you don't have anything, those times when everything seems to be going against you, there's only one guy on your side— and that's the Lord. I feel He gave me the ability to get back to the major leagues; it was acting through Him that enabled me to make it back. Through circumstances which He controlled, my life changed. It was the turning point in my life. As I look back at those times, it was probably the greatest thing that ever happened to me—getting released in Atlanta."

Conversions bring even more glory to Jesus when they include the renewal of a family.

"Faith has been a whole family experience," Paciorek proudly related. His wife, Chris, and he live with their four children in Stone Mountain, Georgia. "We're a unit now. We act as one. We were off a little bit before. It wasn't bad. I'm not saying we didn't have a good life, but there was something definitely lacking."

Putting his faith into action is a daily, conscious opportunity for Paciorek.

"I get a big kick out of applying my faith to others," Paciorek asserted. "I like to help or uplift anybody I come in contact with. All it takes is an occasional pat on the back to lift someone up. I think that is the Lord's plan for all of us—to give to others."

One of the greatest acts of obedience is to share Christ with others. Witnessing as a way of life is simply taking the initiative to share Christ in the power of the Holy Spirit and leaving the results to God.

Paciorek noted that Jesus commissioned Christians to witness for Him when He said, "Therefore go and make disciples in all the nations, baptizing them into the name of the Father and of the Son and of the Holy Spirit, and then teach these new disciples to obey all the commands I have given you; and be sure of this—that I am with you always, even to the end of the world" (Matt. 28:19, 20 TLB).

Another whose thirst was quenched by Christ is Larry Milbourne, a versatile player for the Mariners. Like several of his peers who had achieved the goal of playing major-league baseball, Larry still had a void in his life. Drinking couldn't help him pretend he was happy. Courting pretty girls offered no lasting solution to a nagging thirst.

But Jesus did.

Milbourne, an easygoing native of Port Norris, New Jersey, made the Houston Astros squad in 1974, after four years in the minor leagues. He hit .279 and made the TOPPS All-Rookie team. It was after he met Bob Watson that he ultimately joined Jesus' team.

Watson and Dave Roberts served as spiritual counselors to Milbourne. It took four years for the nurturing seeds to grow, but in 1977 Larry came to know the Lord.

"Before I became a Christian I used to put everything upon myself, and you can't do that. You have to let the Lord take control of your life," Milbourne said.

Like many new Christians, he expected instant success. His career had taken the direction of putting him on the bench for spot duty.

"I expected things to happen right away," Milbourne recalled. "I expected to go out there

143

and see that everything I hit was a base hit. And I expected that everything that was going to happen was going to be good. But I learned it doesn't work like that. I learned that the Christian walk is a gradual process. My walk was slow for a while, but it accelerated as I got to be around other Christians and to share and to have fellowship."

Milbourne, who manager Darrell Johnson hailed as one of baseball's top utility men in 1979, was frank about the temptations of the road—and how his faith helps him.

"Being on the road a lot and being a baseball player can result in having girls hanging around," he asserted. "Satan's going to tempt you that way by having girls hanging around. Ballplayers on the road have a lot of free time, and that prompts Satan to tempt us. But putting faith into the Lord gives me the strength to overcome this temptation."

The same strength is available to all of us. Milbourne noted the Bible passage which reveals how God equips Christians for the battle against Satan. It states: "Put on all of God's armor so that you will be able to stand safe against all strategies and tricks of Satan. For we are not fighting against people made of flesh and blood, but against persons without bodies—the evil rulers of the unseen world, those mighty satanic beings and great evil princes of darkness who rule this world; and against huge numbers of wicked spirits in the spirit world. So use every piece of God's armor to resist the enemy whenever he attacks, and when it is all over, you will still be standing up. But to do this, you will need the strong belt of truth and the breastplate of God's approval. Wear shoes that are able to speed you on as you preach the Good News of peace with God. In every battle you will need faith as your shield to stop the fiery arrows aimed at you by Satan. And you will need the helmet of salvation and the sword of the Spirit—which is the Word of God" (Eph. 6:11-17 TLB).

Ruppert Jones, the first player tabbed by the Seattle franchise at its inception in 1977, agreed with Milbourne about the temptations which stalk ballplayers. Players become idols not only to youngsters—but also to women.

"I'm still not a strong Christian," Jones said candidly. "I'm still an infant, drinking milk instead of eating solid food. I've got my weaknesses. I have to decide the things I don't want to do, the things that can hurt me, and then I must call upon the Lord. He gives me a conscience. If He doesn't bother your conscience, it means you're not one of His children. He helps me."

"Calling upon the Lord is not an option, but a requirement," popular conference speaker

Howard Hendricks once told a sports group.

He said the Bible assists us. It admonishes, "Pray all the time. Ask God for anything in line with the Holy Spirit's wishes. Plead with him, reminding him of your needs, and keep praying earnestly for all Christians everywhere" (Eph. 6:18 TLB).

Jones feels certain his association with athletes from various sports has renewed his faith.

"I just started putting more confidence in Him," Jones said. "He is helping me deal with the game of baseball, deal with my shortcomings and with my successes. He says in the Bible that if you put your trust in Him all the days will be alike instead of one day being good and one day being bad. And that's true. Learning that spiritual truth keeps me on a nice even plane. I know I'm only here to work for the Lord, and that He's working through me. He's making me a better person so I can be a witness and praise His name to other people, and maybe help them a little."

Help a lot—that's what Bruce Bochte's bat did for Seattle in 1978, his first season as a Mariner after signing a free-agent contract. That season and 1977, one which he spent playing for California and Cleveland, were Christian growth years for him.

Bochte, as deliberate in answering questions

as he is swinging a bat, reflected on the question of how his faith has guided his life. He was raised in the Catholic faith but drifted from it in high school. The return to a strong faith was gradual, but steady.

"I think I can say my faith has changed in the sense that it has grown," said Bochte. "I really have a sense that I have received more guidance, particularly in the last year or two. It's made the game of baseball a lot easier; before, it was very difficult for me emotionally."

Bochte, a college star at the University of Santa Clara, where he was drafted by the California Angels in 1972, called his renewed faith a cumulative experience.

"I can't really look back and pick any particular day that turned my life around," he said. "I started my professional career having a great deal of free time, especially on the road. I read some books on religion and on philosophy. After a couple of years of really thinking about it, I decided I wanted to incorporate faith into my life. Since then, it has been a gradual growth."

Pressure tests his faith.

"I know I have a tendency to put a lot of pressure on myself as an individual, which is unhealthy for me spiritually," Bochte shared, as he eyed a bat for his turn at pre-game swings. "On top of that, there are all the outside influences which compound that pressure. It can only eventually get to you. You really don't keep your perspective and follow a prayerful life. I think you really lose contact."

A prayerful life is as important to a Christian as a key is to a car ignition. Without it, you don't get anywhere.

chapter seven

On the surface, Gene Tenace was a success. But the San Diego catcher discovered that not even three world championships brought contentment. Jesus Christ did.

Tenace catapulted to national attention in the 1972 World Series when he hit four home runs, including two in his first two times at bat. He set a World Series record for his slugging percentage that year. His homers equaled a World Series record. For an encore, in 1973 Tenace tied a World Series record for the most bases on balls in a World Series with 11 and the most double plays by a first baseman (4).

But it was after his World Series acclaim that Tenace accepted Jesus Christ. It brought him the contentment which championships failed to bring. It accomplished something money couldn't buy—healthy relationships.

"Winning three world championships is a tremendous feat in itself, but baseball is not my life," Tenace said in a West Coast interview. The Padres, in 1979, figured to battle for the pennant. Instead, they repeated their losing ways, all to the dismay of patient fans.

Tenace has tasted both victory and defeat. He symbolizes the theme that victory on the field cannot compare with the victory of salvation which is "won" through acceptance of Jesus Christ.

No longer does the pressure to produce weigh heavily on Tenace. He has surrendered that to the Lord.

But to him, the greater benefits of his conversion are off the field. "My family is my life and being a Christian is very important to me," Tenace said. "It enables me to get closer to my family. You can play this game for many years but once you take the uniform off you have to have something to fall back on. A lot of players have other income as far as other jobs are concerned. As long as you have faith, something is going to work out for you."

Former A's teammate Sal Bando led Tenace to faith in 1975, after the team's glory years, which featured World Series triumphs in 1972-1974. Bando and Joe Rudi had been inspired to faith by then A's manager, Alvin Dark. Rudi hailed the conversions for saving him and his ex-teammates from a nose dive from victory to uncertainty.

"Sal is a very strict Catholic and he got me to go to Mass with him on different occasions," Tenace related. "It reached the point where I got the message. I took the bull by the horns and talked to my wife; we were willing to get into a church where the entire family could go together."

Believing in the Lord brought Tenace closer to his family. His frankness belies the reality of underlying currents which can rock the private lives of professional athletes.

"My faith really brought our communications back as a family," Tenace said. "Communication is very important to a marriage, or in any other aspect of life. If you have communication with those you're associated with, I think you have a better understanding of one another. This truth has meant a lot to me. Having faith and being able to share my problems with my wife, rather than keeping them all inside, has helped."

Tenace's remarks are candid. A nation remembers him as he gallantly raced around third base on the final stretch of a World Series home-run trot or in his well-publicized contract disputes with Charles O. Finley, owner of the A's. But behind the pedestal on which America puts her athletes, real-life dramas are unfolding, just as they unfold in all Christian lives.

As a sports-crazed nation, does America fail to look at athletes as people who endure the same types of problems and joys as others? Do American sports fans demand performance of athletic ability while ignoring a performer's personal struggles and hurts?

Can fans learn and be inspired from the frankness of Gene Tenace and others as they share their faith, their hurts, their struggles? Can America allow athletes at least one outlet to which they don't have to perform for our entertainment but can share for our benefit?

The most common response from the world, especially from unchurched fans, is to keep sports and religion separate. But how can a Christian keep his faith separate from anything? His faith is his life.

"Fans don't want to hear it," "It's not controversial," are frequent responses to the penetrating questions concerning faith. But who makes that judgment? Usually newspapermen, the same ones who would scream First Amendment rights if a club tried to keep something from their probe. Sportswriters frequently utilize the apropriate "public's right to know" argument in defending what they report. That same principle should apply to all aspects of a player's life which have an impact on his performance.

If a player pulls a hamstring, and that affects his performance, it is reported. If someone— like Tenace, or San Francisco's Jack Clark or

Cincinnati's George Foster—tries to explain on a post-game broadcast how the Lord has strengthened him, fans get silence from the announcer. An active faith is as newsworthy as a pulled hamstring muscle.

An active faith keeps Dave Winfield focused on the right priorities. National press attention tracked him in 1977 in a lingering contract dispute with Padre management. Given less prominence was Winfield's Christian love in the aftermath of a settlement. Winfield sponsored a party for the youth of San Diego, presenting an open house featuring cake and ice cream. It was his way of returning to fans his appreciation and his love for their support.

Good deeds usually are overshadowed in professional sports by the machismo image painted on players by many fans and writers. This is unfortunate, but true.

But for Dave Winfield and other Christian players, the audience is God, not fans. They act to please Him, not writers. They present love to fulfill their Christian promise, not to catch the attention of spectators.

Winfield appreciates his talents, and quickly describes them as "God-given." He was an All-Star football, baseball and basketball player at the University of Minnesota. He was drafted by professional teams in each sport. Winfield could regard his talents as his own. Often in life we depend on our own capabilities, forgetting it is Jesus who gives the power for achievement.

But Winfield doesn't forget.

"I think that no matter what happens on the field I can be strong enough to feel it isn't the most important thing in my life," Winfield said. "It is here and now. Baseball is my occupation, and I want to do well, but I feel that if I didn't have any money and couldn't play baseball, I'd still have love for people. It is easy to say because I am doing well, but I feel these are my principles."

Love. It is the heart of Christianity. It is a trait which makes base hits or strikeouts seem irrelevant.

The Bible says it like this, "If I had the gift of being able to speak in other languages without learning them, and could speak in every language there is in all of heaven and earth, but didn't love others, I would only be making noise. If I had the gift of prophecy and knew all about what is going to happen in the future, knew everything about everything, but didn't love others, what good would it do? Even if I had the gift of faith so that I could speak to a mountain and make it move, I would still be worth nothing at all without love" (1 Cor. 13:1, 2 TLB).

Love guides the life of Padre infielder Bill Almon. He had every reason to be discouraged when the 1979 season opened. He had lost his starting job, and had been relegated to the bench. But his faith held steadfast.

Almon, signed for a reported $100,000 bonus in 1974, spent four seasons in the minor leagues before climbing to San Diego in 1977. He promptly led the National League shortstops in total chances with 882 and in sacrifice hits with 20. But 1979 presented a different view—one from the bench.

"Being a Christian helps me both in the good and bad times," Almon said. "I feel that the Lord will never give me more than I can handle so I figure as bad as times can get I must be able to handle it because He wouldn't give me more than I can handle."

Don Reynolds, another reserve player for the Padres, also banks on his faith to enable him to endure the joys and disappointments. Reynolds climbed to the big leagues in 1978 after three seasons in Triple-A minor-league ball.

"I think my Christian background is really helping me because it gives me strength when times aren't going good," Reynolds described. "It also lets me keep a level head when I'm having success—not only in baseball but in life as a person."

Though raised in a Christian home, Reynolds's faith blossomed as an adult. He noted the spiritual truth that we do not automatically become Christians because our parents are. We cannot claim salvation through their faith. We each must invite the Lord into our hearts and allow Him to be chief resident in our lives. We must let Christ be the guide not only in our hearts, but in every room of our lives.

"For a long time I thought I was a Christian but I really wasn't," Reynolds said. "I went to church occasionally as a youngster, but mostly because my mother took me. I wasn't going because I necessarily wanted to go; I went because I had to."

Friends in high school, though, impressed on Reynolds the need to have a personal, day-to-day relationship with Jesus.

"I got to thinking and realized I wanted God to lead my life," he recalled. "I wanted Him to take over my life and to run it for me because I wasn't doing a real good job trying to do it on my own."

His faith helps him in the temptations which face single baseball players. The "limelight" of sports elevates a person's stature. Along with it come opportunities in several social areas.

"Being single, I have my share of temptations, not only sexually, but also from feelings of being lonely," Reynolds candidly shared. "I think because of what God is doing in my life I don't have the desire to go out and chase women. I'm not implying that I stay in my room and hide. I just don't have the desires for a lot of things which most people think single, professional athletes want."

Most images of public figures, from athletes to actors, focus on the lure of sexual and worldly temptation. Some sports books capitalize on the indiscretions of a few but ignore the opposite— the strength to resist temptation provided by Jesus Christ.

The latter might not make good reading for some. But it makes for good lives.

Though it is an adage in most parts of America, it is a truism in Philadelphia. The hopes of spring can turn to the frustrations of fall.

On the wave of their first National League pennant since 1950, the Phillies squandered the opportunity three consecutive times from 1976-1978. Though nabbing the Eastern Division crown, the Phillies were thwarted in the playoffs, twice by the Dodgers in come-from-behind victories.

Frustration is exhibited in many ways. For Mike Schmidt, one of baseball's most feared power hitters, it has been displayed in converse fashions. The letdown tracked him after the 1977 season. But after the 1978 disappointment, Schmidt handed his letdown to the Lord.

Kneeling near a batting cage, watching the opposition practice, Schmidt discussed how he became a new man after accepting Jesus Christ on January 9, 1978.

The thrill of three home run derby titles had brought him only artificial happiness. Schmidt intimidates pitchers. Between 1974-1978, he belted 171 homers, the most of any big leaguer during the same period, including Reggie Jackson, Dave Kingman and George Foster. He belted nearly fifty in 1979.

As talented with his glove at third base as he is with his bat at the plate, Schmidt has been a regular All-Star and Gold Glove winner. His success brings a salary commensurate with his accomplishments.

How could life be better?

Schmidt learned the answer one cold, snowy day in 1978 when he surrendered his life to Jesus Christ. Mike Schmidt, the feared hitter, became a changed man. He still intimidates pitchers with his bat. But his priorities are rearranged, putting Christ and his family ahead of his baseball achievements.

Schmidt said about the road to his conversion, "The general feeling of getting high on success and on the earthly things was occurring in my life. Given a great deal of money to play the game of baseball, I was a pretty materialistic guy. I think all of my energies were channeled in the wrong direction."

But friends outside of baseball showed him and his wife, Donna, another way. This was the way through Jesus Christ.

Mike's conversion was gradual. "There were no fireworks," he recalled. "As friends talked about God, I questioned Christianity and I questioned the Bible, reading a lot about it. I wrestled with it until that January day when I gave my life to Christ. I still have a long way to go."

Schmidt noted that the Lord deals with us where we are. When we search, He is there. When we believe, He is there. When we slip, He is there. As we grow, He is there.

"Slowly but surely my perspective of life and my relationship with my wife improved," Schmidt said, maintaining his kneeling position while watching batting practice. "I began to experience the feeling of unselfishness and generosity and all the good things associated with Christianity."

The biggest change in his life, he described, was his attitude toward life and other people. He grasped the reality that God gave him his ability and put him in a Phillies uniform for a purpose. His appreciation and gratitude for the Lord's grace multiplied.

"Just in general, giving my life to the Lord is more fun," Mike said. "Jesus says, 'I give you life and I give it to you abundantly.' I'm learning how true that is."

Pressures on athletes can be immense, especially if they are media superstars. Fan expectation is great. A player has a tendency to raise his own expectation. Schmidt knows that all too well.

"I've been the best player in the league and I think I've been the worst player in the league," he said. "I've been on both sides of the spectrum. But through God, I've learned to draw strength in times of suffering, and down times, and testing times. People who know the Lord can handle tests and setbacks in life."

Schmidt also notes that the media develop a secular image for ballplayers, one which usually depicts them collectively as greedy, uneducated playboys.

Can Christian athletes counter this image?

"About all we can do as Christian athletes is try to eliminate pride, trying to give credit where it belongs—to the Lord," Schmidt responded. "The credit should be given to Christ for everything that happens to us in this game. When we need to talk about Christianity is during the down times, the testing times, the times of trouble. We need to hold our heads up high and show we can take the bad with the good. That's when we make our greatest endorsement for Jesus Christ."

Schmidt's career has known its share of down times. Signed in the free-agent draft in 1971 after earning his degree in business administration from Ohio University, Schmidt spent only one full year in the minors. He batted .291 with 26 homers at Eugene in 1972. But his climb to the major leagues was less than an instant success. His 1973 rookie season produced 18 home runs but only a .196 batting average.

Those are the types of "downs" which Jesus uses to "lift" a player's attitude.

Still eyeing batting practice with the same intensity as when he began to share his faith, Schmidt reflected on what brings him satisfaction in his Christian walk.

"I think the most satisfaction comes from admitting I'm a Christian and standing up for it. I haven't had anybody come up to me and say that because of my stand for Christ he gave his life to Jesus. When that happens, I think it will be the ultimate in reward."

Bob Boone stands up for the Lord. Boone, the Phillies chapel leader, came to a personal relationship with Jesus as a result of the influences of Baseball Chapel. Bob, the son of former Detroit Tiger first baseman Ray Boone, is another well-educated athlete. He attended Stanford University. A native of San Diego, California, he was drafted by the Phillies in 1969 as a pitcher-third baseman. But he was switched to the position of catcher in 1970, helping him rise to the big leagues in 1973.

Boone, who makes his home in Medford, New

Jersey, with his wife, Susan, and their two sons, broke Johnny Bench's ten-year hold on the Gold Glove for catchers in 1978, winning the coveted honor with a .991 fielding percentage. He committed just six errors in 129 games.

Boone said he was "roped into being the team's chapel leader" in 1976 because of his role as player representative.

"I was asked to try to line up speakers, and I thought that would be fine," Bob said. It turned out to be more than fine. It turned out to be life-altering.

"We started having tremendous speakers from all walks of life come and witness or give us a message," Boone recalled. "It started me thinking and reading about the Christian faith. I got into a Bible study and began learning about God's Word, and about what God wants from us."

Shortly thereafter, he surrendered his life to Jesus Christ.

"I had always thought I believed in God and in Jesus Christ, but I had been running my own life," Boone reflected. "I still had the reins of my life in my hands. When I surrendered them to God, that was an important step in my life."

Like Mike Schmidt, his attitudes toward life and baseball underwent a dramatic transformation. Life became more enjoyable. Life developed a purpose. Pressures, burdens and worries were tossed into God's lap.

"I think I still live about the same life I did before," Bob said. "I still sin, though I try not to; I'm conscious of trying not to sin, but I realize I'm human and I'm going to make a lot of mistakes, and on a daily basis. But I know when I pray for forgiveness, I'm forgiven. That in itself gives me a tremendous lift."

The Bible puts it like this: "Each of us must bear some faults and burdens of his own. For none of us is perfect!" (Gal. 6:5 TLB).

"I consider myself a baby Christian," Boone said. "I'm just now starting to grow. But the main thing is that the belief is there, the prayer is there, and the commitment is there. I'm learning to let Jesus take control and guide me."

Another Phillie who is guided by Jesus is Garry Maddox, a Gold Glove center fielder for four consecutive seasons. He also is one of baseball's most consistent hitters with a lifetime average of .294.

Maddox, acquired from San Francisco in 1975 for Willie Montanez, signed with the Giants organization in 1968, but was promptly drafted into the military. He spent a two-year hitch in the army, including a one-year tour of Vietnam. The stark realities which a war magnifies brought Garry to his faith.

"I didn't have an experience which scared me

to death," he recalled. "I came to my senses and realized I had to set up my life and give it some direction."

Maddox befriended a soldier who was a Christian. "He helped me immensely." Garry was baptized in Vietnam.

His faith wavered during times of prosperity resulting from his baseball success, Maddox said. But he grew in faith after engaging in Bible studies in 1977.

Maddox noted that more players are turning to Jesus.

"With the big salaries, players discover that money's not everything," he offered. "You can go through your entire life wanting and as soon as you get it you find out it can't cure any sickness that might develop in your family, or that emptiness still dominates."

Maddox, who lives in West Berlin, New Jersey, with his wife, Sondra, and two sons, is active during the off-season, frequently contributing his energies in fund-raising activities for the Philadelphia Child Guidance Clinic.

He believes in the Bible admonishment, "Faith by itself, if it has no works, is dead" (James 2:17 RSV).

An active faith is important to Jim Kaat, one of baseball's all-time winners, with a lifetime record of 261-217 entering the 1979 season, his twentieth in the major leagues. He was playing cards with several teammates in the locker room before our interview. He was suddenly summoned by Manager Danny Ozark. Ozark had some news: Kaat had been sold to the New York Yankees.

But not even the suddenness of events—he was ticketed to fly out of San Francisco four hours after the announcement—could keep Kaat from sharing how Jesus Christ has guided his life.

A native of Zeeland, Michigan, Kaat was signed by the old Washington Senators in 1957. When the Senators moved to Minnesota to become the Twins in 1961, he went along. A rookie season of 9-17 didn't discourage him. In his most successful season—1966—Jim won twenty-five and lost thirteen. But he also "won" the biggest decision of his life—he accepted Jesus Christ.

Though raised in a strong Christian home, Kaat said he never made a personal commitment until that season, when pitching coach, Al Worthington, taught Jim more than how to throw a baseball.

"Al was an example of what a Christian should be," Kaat recalled. "He had a lot of influence on me. I made the decision that year to accept Christ as my Savior, not as just a great figure in history."

After twelve-and-one-half seasons with the

Twins, he was traded to Chicago's White Sox, where he posted consecutive 20-win seasons in 1974-75. The Sox traded him to the Phillies in 1976. He brought his record-breaking fielding talent to the National League. From 1962 to 1977, Kaat set a record sixteen consecutive Gold Gloves as the top fielding pitcher—fourteen years in the American League and two in the National League.

"A few years ago, when players heard about the Fellowship of Christian Athletes, they promptly thought of someone who gave up smoking and who was an All-American," Kaat recalled. "But we've come to realize that you don't have to fit into any particular mold to live the Christian life. Regardless of your background, Jesus is a loving God. I think more players are realizing now that it is their faith that helps them through the bad times and gives them peace during both the bad and good times."

Still, some players are reluctant to profess their faith to a public which already puts them in the limelight.

"It seems that whenever someone finds out that an athlete is taking a stand for Christ, they make a national thing out of it, which in and of itself is all right. But most of the public then reacts by imposing a standard which they expect that player to live up to. But, being sinful, the player, or anyone, is unable to live up to the arbitrary standard. We're just mortal beings."

A visitor into the Pittsburgh Pirates locker room could mistakenly have taken the Pirates for being in first place if the standings hadn't belied the truth.

On a warm July afternoon, Pirate players possessed that frequent descriptive cliché: they were loose.

What it means in practice is that players talk to one another. Horseplay is accepted and tolerated. The game is left on the field, not dragged into the clubhouse and replayed.

There are few teams in major-league baseball with the camaraderie of the Pirates. Houston is one. Montreal is another. The Chicago White Sox are the American League's most relaxed team.

"Hanging loose" doesn't guarantee championships. The New York Yankees, Los Angeles Dodgers and old Oakland A's are teams which have sported superiority on the field despite friction in the clubhouse. But a camaraderie survives longer than winning—and losing.

A relaxed team seems better able to accept the diversity of personalities which comprise major-league clubs. On the Pittsburgh team, many personalities are dominating.

One who tries to let his life style speak for him

is Bill Robinson, a Pennyslvania native who has played most of his career in his home state, first for the Phillies for three seasons before a 1975 trade to Pittsburgh. Robinson has experienced both sides of the cross-state rivalry. The Pirates and Phillies dominated the National League East in the seventies, with the Phillies winning the title in 1976, 1977, and 1978. The Pirates won the National League pennant in 1979 and beat the Baltimore Orioles in the dramatic seven-game World Series.

Bill Robinson's best year was in 1977—both on and off the field. He batted .304 with twenty-six home runs. And he was born again, following in the footsteps of his mother, who accepted Jesus Christ as her Savior five years earlier. Mrs. Robinson is the only woman to ever address Baseball Chapel services.

Robinson's conversion culminated from seeing how his mother's faith in Jesus had changed her life. He longed for the same assurance and confidence.

"I asked the Lord to come into my life and to save my soul," Robinson recalled before a July game. Many new believers expect a dramatic bolt in the sky. Bill Robinson was one of them.

"I kind of expected some macho hand to come down and just grab me by the throat and say, 'Hey, I've got you now; it's all over for you.' But it doesn't happen like that."

Robinson's conversion, as it has done for millions before him, produced new priorities.

"I feel that He controls me," Robinson said. "I don't worry as much as I once did. If I go 5-for-5 and am fortunate enough to get on a radio interview, the first words from my lips are praise for the Lord. I owe everything to Him."

How about 0-for-4?

"I am able to accept that too because I've given my performance to the Lord," Robinson said.

He shared how his focus has changed. "People have to have some direction—direction from the Lord," he asserted. "There's more to life than making a million dollars. I don't care about being a superstar. My superstar is my father, who worked thirty years in a steel mill. It almost killed him with a heart attack. I've learned, through Christ, to put things in their proper perspective."

Robinson, like Maddox in Philadelphia and several other sports figures, puts his faith to work during the off-season. Robinson is chairman of the Lupus Society, which helps fight lupus erythematosus, a rheumatic disease which affects 500,000 Americans. He also sponsors an annual celebrity golf tourament to raise funds to help the society continue its search to find answers in hopes of eliminating the disease.

"I fully realize that this time we spend on earth is nothing compared to what's in store for us in heaven," said Robinson.

Tim Foli, the Pirates' shortstop, learned that too.

"My wife and I had been searching," Foli recalled. "We knew there was a God and we knew He had control but we just didn't know how to give Him control."

An evangelical sports conference in San Diego in October of 1977 taught Foli how to surrender control to the Lord.

He learned "that there are so many things in the Bible that pertain to everyday life. You just don't realize it until you really dig into the Bible. The Word is like the rulebook and you know we have to play by a rulebook in baseball; life has its rulebook too, and it's the Bible. It doesn't mean that you follow it word for word, because we're human beings and we're not that good. But by having Christ in our lives, by accepting Him, He takes our sins and all we have to do is to ask for forgiveness and He'll take care of those things that we do wrong, and help us to grow."

Cynics are quick to look for a Christian to stumble. It frequently starts a barrage of, "I thought you were a Christian."

Foli knows that all too well. He was suspended for five days near the end of the 1978 season following an altercation with Dick Ruthven in Atlanta.

Foli, though, realized he isn't perfect. He knows he will fall short of the standard of Christ from time to time. But he has something which nonbelievers don't possess—an assurance of forgiveness through confession to Jesus Christ.

About the cynics, Foli said, "The biggest thing is to hope that some day they see the truth before they die so they too can have everlasting life. The number two hope is that they see the truth so they too can get that peace of mind that God promises. Everybody in baseball is pretty well financially set, but that doesn't make a person happy. It doesn't make a lawyer happy. It doesn't make a businessman happy. We tend to think we can get peace of mind from material things. Once you have them, though, you realize that that's not really where it's at. It's with Jesus."

Foli was born in 1950 in Culver City, California. He turned down football scholarships at USC and Notre Dame to sign with the Mets in 1968. After only three minor-league seasons, he earned a spot with New York but was traded to Montreal in 1972. After five seasons with the Expos, Foli was traded to San Francisco. After one year there, the Mets repurchased him in 1978 but dealt him to

Pittsburgh after the 1979 season started.

Trades can be frustrating. After a player gets his family settled, a trade can erase the security of new friendships. But even those worries can be surrendered.

"There's no question that since I accepted Christ into my life and let Him work through me, He's taken care of some of the things I tried to take care of before but couldn't," Foli said. "Baseball hasn't always been roses for me. But I trust in God's plan and I know that by trusting in His plan that He's going to give me the peace of mind that we're all searching for anyway."

Put another way, Foli views the trades, the successes and the failures from one perspective: "Having faith allows you to realize that if things are going to happen, they're going to happen. We do the best we can and try to give the Holy Spirit control."

Manny Sanguillen, a native of Colon, Panama, surrendered the control of his life to the Holy Spirit in 1964 at the age of twenty. It was about the same time that he signed with the Pirates as a free agent. Sanguillen is the only player in baseball history to be traded for a manager. The Pirates dealt him to the Oakland A's in 1977 for Manager Chuck Tanner. But Sanguillen returned "home" after one season, when Pittsburgh reacquired him for three players.

Sanguillen, in eleven major league seasons,

has enjoyed the success which catchers dream about. His lifetime average in 1979 was .300. He was secure financially and in the Lord Jesus.

Sanguillen's priorities, even in the face of success as measured by human standards, remain unchanged. His goal is to help people by returning a portion of the "good life" to them. Like many Christian players, Sanguillen doesn't bank on *his* talents—he banks on the talents which the Lord allows him to have.

Sanguillen helped start a baseball program at Pan American Bible School. There were no cheers. There were no fans. But Manny was playing for an audience of one—the Lord. He prayed about how he could best help the youngsters in his homeland.

As a veteran player whose career dates back to an era before the big sports dollars, Sanguillen has seen how large salaries have controlled many of his teammates.

"They love the money," he observed. "We are here to live in a lot of different ways. The Lord blesses us differently. He says, though, that as you give, you receive. You ask, and in obedience to Him, you receive. If you really love the Lord and you have faith, it isn't how much money that becomes important. It's how to use it to glorify God. It's learning to share. It's learning to give."

Manny Sanguillen gives. And because of it, youngsters learn about baseball—and the Lord!

Matt Alexander learned about the Lord while growing up in Shreveport, Louisiana. His faith helps him to accept his unusual role in baseball—he's a pinch runner. But pinch runners are a new phenomenon. It is rare for a team to employ a player for virtually that reason alone.

Consequently, team acceptance comes harder. Most players have a dim view of a player whose contributions are limited. Alexander first found himself in that category with the Chicago Cubs in 1973.

His toughest climb for acceptance, though, came in Oakland when he played (or ran) for the A's from 1975 to 1977. Though appearing in 214 games, Alexander swung the bat only eighty-two times. But during this period he stole sixty-three bases.

One who likes pinch runners is Chuck Tanner. After Tanner came to Pittsburgh in the Sanguillen trade, he signed Alexander as a free agent. All over again, Alexander waited for acceptance by his teammates.

"I've learned to accept the position I'm in," Alexander said. "I've learned to be patient. I pray for everything—even my failures."

Though the acceptance of teammates migh waver, Alexander is secure because of his faith.

"The Bible says that Jesus is the same today, tomorrow and forever," Alexander affirms. That makes "hanging loose" a lot less difficult.

chapter eight

The test of faith is how it endures when things go poorly.

For the Los Angeles Dodgers, 1979 was among the club's worst seasons since coming to the West Coast from New York in 1958. From back-to-back pennants, the Dodgers stumbled to third place in the National League's Western Division.

Line drives which years before had whizzed by the outstretched arms of infielders for base hits seemed to go directly at fielders in 1979. Balls which the wind might have aided in seasons past for a home run seemed to die at the fence, enabling outfielders to catch them.

For many players, the discouragement of 1979 could have been crippling. But for Dusty Baker, the Dodgers' left fielder, there is glory in Jesus Christ even in the gloom of an off-season.

"Ever since I was a little kid, God has been good to me," Baker shared as he donned his spikes for a pre-game warm-up. Baker, in his eighth season, was as enthusiastic for the games as he was when the Atlanta Braves tabbed him as their starting left fielder in 1972 after five minor-league seasons. Baker, a native of Riverside, California, was traded to the Dodgers in 1976.

Reflecting on the disappointment of the 1979 season, Baker focused on the Lord. "Different things have happened in my life to prove that God is real and alive. If it wasn't for God, I wouldn't be here in baseball now."

Baker recalled that after a year at American River Junior College in Sacramento, California, he was weighing the chance to attend the University of Santa Clara. At the same time, he was drafted by the Atlanta Braves.

"A lot of people then, and before, told me I couldn't make it in the big leagues," Baker recalled. "They all said I was too skinny, I was too this and too that. But I had faith in God. Before I signed with the Braves, I prayed the night before, seeking God's guidance. I didn't know whether to sign or to go to Santa Clara."

Baker signed. And his critics, masquerading as friends, still second-guessed his decision.

"Everybody told me I had made the wrong move, and that I was foolish," Baker said. "But as it turned out, my career has progressed exactly the way God had it planned."

In 1977, Baker hit .291, drove in 86 runs and hit 30 homers. He teamed up with Steve Garvey, Reggie Smith and Ron Cey to set a major-league record—they were the first foursome on any team to hit 30 or more homers each in the same season.

Baker treated success with the same style he had treated disappointment a season earlier—with humbleness and a sense of purpose.

"What gives me the most satisfaction," Baker said, "is that when things seem darkest, Christ has always come through, like in the nick of time. It's hard to explain specific instances, but it has happened probably ten to twenty times in my life."

Baker was reared in a Christian home but came to a personal commitment to Jesus when he was thirteen. He too strayed from his faith in high school, falling to the temptations of the world.

"I started drifting like a lot of people do," Baker recalled. "But when I got into my late teens and early twenties, I came back to Christ. It was too hard without Him. For a lot of things I had to depend on myself for strength, and that just wasn't sufficient to help me through. It reached the point that I couldn't stand it any more because I was on my own. I had nothing to lean on but Dusty."

Steve Garvey has leaned on God for his

strength. His life style is frequently a target for cynics. On a Los Angeles radio talk show after the 1978 All-Star game in which Garvey was named the most valuable player, an announcer asked listeners to call him on this topic: "Is Steve Garvey perfect?"

The announcer described Garvey as having a beautiful wife, a pure life style and immense baseball talent. The program reflected a cynicism which was evident even to the naive. America's moral standards and expectations are so low that many seek to mock those who rise above them.

"From the time I became a Catholic and received Communion and baptism, my Christianity has been an all-encompassing part of my life," Garvey said. "I know I am a child of God and that He has a plan for me."

Garvey, a native of Tampa, was drafted by the Dodgers in 1968 out of Michigan State University. Garvey's major-leagues start seemed inauspicious. It took him until 1973 to win a starting job. Since then, however, he has been a fixture at first base.

Garvey shared how his faith helps him on the field, especially in the throes of 1979's frustrations.

"It takes away a lot of anxiety and pressures, knowing that I have Jesus Christ and that I am trying to be the person He wants me to be,"

Garvey said. "By trying to do that, I give 100 percent of myself both on and off the field, to my family and to other people."

Another who looks to the Lord for his strength is Don Sutton, Los Angeles's all-time winning pitcher with 205 wins in thirteen seasons entering 1979.

"I realize that my career is the result of some natural gifts God has given me plus the help of other people who have been there to help me along," Sutton asserted.

Sutton's career has had its share of peaks and valleys, including a ten-week stretch without a victory in 1974, though he finished with nineteen wins and the Dodgers won a division title.

Sutton learned a valuable lesson. "When we are sustained by our friends and by God, we can endure a lot of pain and disappointment. Ultimately we know things will improve."

Fitting into God's plans was a new experience for Dodger Bill Russell in 1976. Like a youngster still savoring the joy of a new experience, Russell was outspoken about how his faith revolutionized his life.

"My life has changed in all respects," he said. "It has made my marriage a lot better. I've become more patient with the kids and I want to teach them about the Lord in the right way. I wasn't raised in a Christian atmosphere but I want my kids to háve one."

Russell's wife, Mary Ann, was raised in a Christian home and she helped guide Bill to the Lord.

"In baseball, you're away from your family a lot, and you're lonely," Russell said. "Your wife gets lonely when you're gone too. We look more and more to the Lord and the Bible at these times. As a result, the Lord has brought us closer together."

Old-fashioned donnybrooks which occasionally erupt in baseball are long remembered. But there are many players who have prayed for the Lord to curb their tempers.

"There are so many things that happen in baseball that occasionally your temper flares, and it's tough to control it," Russell noted. "Things happen during the game and pressures mount. But I think if you can settle down and let the Lord take you into His hands and run your life, then everything will be all right."

Russell, whose Dodger career began in 1970, has observed the press over the years. An error to a ballplayer is part of the game. It can become a cause célèbre to a writer, an opportunity to write pointedly. Russell sees the growing Christian movement in sports as an opportunity for players to set examples to writers and other followers of the game.

"They need to see that we're not the macho

types they think we are," Russell said. "We're human beings and we believe in God. We can set an example not only for them but also for people who are struggling and think they can go out and drink and smoke and take their dope and have a good time. They're really missing something. We, as professional ballplayers, can set an example—a Christian example."

Russell's enthusiasm was refreshing. His faith, he said, "brings me satisfaction in knowing that God cares for us. He died for our sins. Just think, somebody went through what He went through for us. You've really got to love the guy who does something like that. You've really got to believe in Him."

Russell hurriedly left the clubhouse for the playing field. Smiling!

Bruce Sutter has been among baseball's top relief pitchers since mid-1976. But it was an injury which changed his life.

Sutter is another in the long list of baseball players who credit Baseball Chapel—and Dave Roberts—for their faith. The Chicago Cubs right hander was having the type of season which players dream about in 1977. He saved nearly every Cub victory.

"It seemed like everything was just going right," Sutter recalled. "Everything was coming easy. I was pitching well, then all of a sudden I got injured. I was out for a long time. In 1978, I started the season off the same way, when all of a sudden I couldn't get anybody out for about seven weeks. I didn't feel good at all."

Roberts had an answer, one which he has shared with numerous players on several teams. The answer was Jesus Christ.

Sutter had been moving toward a commitment when Roberts shared his faith. "Without chapel, I think it would have been difficult for me to make a commitment," Sutter said. "But by attending since I came to the big leagues in 1976, I gradually learned. And I would hear something said which I wanted to know more about. I found myself looking things up in the Bible."

Sutter's 1977 season, despite missing a month with a muscle injury, was one of the best ever for a relief hurler—31 saves and seven wins. In 1978, Sutter posted 27 saves and eight victories. In 1979 he won the Cy Young award.

Sutter shared his faith with his wife, who rededicated herself to the Lord. "My family life is better and my overall outlook on life has improved," he said.

Sutter's roommate, pitcher Rick Reuschel, also was touched by Roberts, who played for the Cubs for only one season, 1978. Reuschel credits Roberts with reviving his faith.

"It has made me a little more tolerant of other

people and situations that come along in baseball," Reuschel said. "It's easier to cope with problems."

Steve Dillard, acquired by the Cubs from Detroit in May of 1979, is a player whom teammates seek out for their questions about the Lord. Dillard's strong love for Jesus makes him a spiritual leader on the Cubs.

After an outstanding collegiate career at the University of Mississippi, including a spot on the College World Series All-Star team, Dillard signed with the Boston Red Sox. After five minor-league seasons, he became a reserve player for Boston in 1977. But he was traded to Detroit in 1978, then to the Cubs.

"This is my third team in three years, and it has been tough in many ways," Dillard shared. "We didn't know whether to buy a home in Chicago or not, so my wife and I prayed about it, seeking the Lord to guide us." Dillard bought the house.

Dillard said his faith became all-encompassing in 1972. "I realized that Christ wants two things from us—He wants us to give ourselves to Him so we can receive eternal life, and He wants us to enjoy the abundant life He has given us here on earth."

Dillard has seen players on three teams come to the Lord. Commenting on the growing number, he said, "I think one reason is that many of the fellows come out of high school without ever having had any money or material things. They make the big leagues and start to make considerable salaries. They think material goods are what they've been looking for, but then they realize that doesn't provide the answer to contentment. They have money and material possessions but they don't have true happiness or peace. Then they see some Christian ballplayers and realize there is something different about them. They check into it, and many come to accept the Lord."

During the off-season, Dillard frequently attends a Pro Athletes Outreach conference, which is designed to teach athletes how to share their faith in Jesus Christ.

"The last one was in St. Petersburg," Dillard said. "We went out to a drug rehabilitation clinic where some of the players spoke, then divided into groups. With all the political scandals, athletes are about the last group of people kids look up to at all. That's the purpose of Pro Athletes Outreach—to share Christ with youngsters."

Living a Christian life style is tough, Dillard tells youngsters. There's nothing easy about it. But there is a consistent, unchanging focal point—Jesus Christ.

Dillard shares with youngsters, "You're going to lose your temper every now and then, but that doesn't mean you're not a Christian. We're going to make mistakes. But God loves us. And I don't care how strong a Christian you are, you will worry sometimes. At those times, just pause to think about what Jesus would do in the situation. First, he would talk to the Father about it and then be patient. That's what we should do too."

Tim Blackwell, a reserve catcher for the Cubs, can attest that living a Christian life is difficult but rewarding.

He candidly discussed his struggles. "I have a tendency to look for God's guidance in times of need but when things are going pretty good, I pat myself on the back. Now I'm learning how to make my faith a day-to-day way of life and how to turn things over to the Lord."

Dillard's trade to the Cubs was hailed by Blackwell. Both played for the Red Sox in 1977 and their wives are friends. Blackwell looks to Dillard for spiritual counsel and they are able to give Christian support to each other.

Watching the lives of born-again players—like anyone—can be disillusioning at times unless we maintain a proper perspective, realizing that a Christian will stumble and sin.

Mike Krukow, a promising starting pitcher on the Cubs said, "I used to see guys who were born-again Christians and I'd watch them. And they'd always falter. I always became bummed out at this until I realized that these guys aren't perfect. I learned you don't have to be good to become a Christian—you become a Christian for help to become good."

Baseball Chapel services challenged Krukow, a six-feet-four native of Long Beach.

"I learned what it means to be a Christian. It has sure slowed me down. And it's given my life some serenity and guidance which I sorely needed."

This is available for everyone—through faith.

On June 7, 1972, Dave Roberts ended a brilliant collegiate career at Oregon University, signed a contract with the San Diego Padres and was in the starting lineup the same day.

Roberts—who is unrelated to the Dave Roberts who has pitched for several teams— played 100 major-league games that season, hitting .244 with five homers. The bright career predicted for him as the first player chosen in the baseball draft that year was off and running.

But his is not a success story—not in athletic terms, that is.

"I had some immediate success my first couple of years, but then I had a bad season in

1974 and I've been an extra man on teams ever since," Roberts said.

He was traded from San Diego to Texas after the 1978 season. The Rangers used Roberts as a utility player.

Many players would be crushed by what has happened to Roberts. But he hasn't been because of his faith in Jesus Christ, a faith that developed in high school.

Each time Roberts had seemingly earned a spot on the San Diego roster, he was sent back to the minor leagues. On four occasions San Diego sent him back to their minor-league team in Hawaii.

"Each time my wife and I would search the Bible for strength and words of encouragement," Roberts recalled in an interview one day after his pinch-hit homer enabled Texas to beat Oakland. "What really helps us is the passage in Psalm 37 where the Psalmist says that a man's steps are established by the Lord when he delights in His way."

For Dave Roberts, it means that when he falls, he isn't hurled head first. He has God to lift him up.

"I have ambitions and plans, and there are things I strive for and hopefully will accomplish. But I realize that the Lord has set my steps. While on one hand I'm responsible for my actions, on the other, God directs my steps. I'm not in control of my ultimate destiny—He's the one who guides me." Even to the minor leagues.

Roberts strived for a professional athletic career while growing up in Eugene, Oregon. "All of my ambitions were directed towards becoming a baseball player. In high school, through a series of circumstances, I turned my life around. I got into God's Word and began to understand His promises."

"Now," Roberts said, "my goal in sports and in life is to become more Christlike. I think by doing that it can make me a better ballplayer, a better person, a better husband, and just about a better anything. That may sound strange in the world of athletics to have a ballplayer say I'm trying to become more Christlike. What that means is doing your work heartily as unto the Lord rather than for men. It's doing things as Jesus would do them."

Following Jesus has been Ferguson Jenkins's walk since 1972, his seventh season in an illustrative career which featured 231 wins entering the 1979 season, including six consecutive 20-game seasons with the Chicago Cubs from 1967 to 1972.

The Texas right-hander, a lean six-feet-five, 210-pound native of Chatham, Ontario, Canada, won a career-high twenty-five games in his first season with Texas in 1974.

The death of Jenkins's mother in 1970

weighed heavily on him for two years. "I was close to her and I felt hurt that she had been taken away. It took me two years to sit down and talk to the Lord."

That "talk" brought Jenkins to the Lord.

During that era in baseball, few Christian players professed their faith to one another, let alone to the public. Jenkins has watched the evangelical explosion in the big leagues ever since.

"I don't mind being exposed as being a Christian," Jenkins asserted. "I'm proud of it."

So is Jim Sundberg, Texas' All-Star catcher who reached the major leagues in 1974 after just ninety-one minor-league games in 1973. He was picked for the American League All-Star team in his rookie season. He won Gold Glove awards, for being behind the plate, from 1976 to 1978.

Like Roberts, Sundberg climbed from college—University of Iowa—into baseball. But unlike Roberts, he has stayed in the major leagues as a starter.

Also like Roberts, Sundberg draws on God's power to help him. "With the stress and strain of 162 games, I go to the Lord and ask Him for the strength to play through the season," Sundberg said. "If it wasn't for the Lord, I wouldn't have the strength."

Chapel services put Sundberg back into

fellowship with the Lord to the point where he was team chapel leader in 1979. He has a three-step plan to help others from straying from their faith in high school or college like he did.

"In order to keep our faith, there are three things we must do," Sundberg said. "One is to read the Bible because it's the only way the Lord will speak to us. We must pray regularly because it's the only way we can talk to Him. And we must have fellowship with other Christians because that gives us strength and guidance. These three steps will keep you in fellowship with the Lord and enable you to grow."

Even in the major leagues!

chapter nine

Pat Kelly's career in 1975 was at a stage familiar to many veterans. He had money in the bank, a fancy car, several possessions, and a nagging feeling that despite it all, there must be more to life.

Kelly, a key veteran on the surging Baltimore Orioles, reflected, "I was also going through some emotional changes because I had fallen in love for the first time. My nerves began to get fouled up, and my mind became distorted. It was then that God began to deal with my mind and my nervous system. And this is what it took to humble me. God began to deal with my heart."

Soon, there emerged a new, relaxed, loving Kelly. His leadership on a young 1979 team played a key behind-the-scenes role. Kelly knows there are ways to help a team beyond simply using a bat.

Baltimore's teams during the later 1970s

attracted critics who questioned why the Orioles couldn't repeat their banner years of 1969-1974, which included five division titles and World Series appearances in 1969-1971. Though the national press focuses on Boston and New York, Baltimore has recorded the best record of any Eastern Division club during the 1970s.

The Orioles each year are said to be rebuilding. In 1979, manager Earl Weaver "rebuilt" quickly by blending youth with veterans like Jim Palmer, Ken Singleton and Kelly to win the American League pennant in the playoffs against California.

Kelly, in a West Coast interview, shared his conversion. "I now realize," he said, "that God wants to deal with our hearts and minds. This is what He wants changed. When your heart and your mind begin to change, then God can start to deal with you."

Like many baby Christians, Kelly expected instant change after his born-again experience in 1975. But it didn't develop that way.

"You know, I just wanted to take a pill, and hope the next day all my problems would be solved," Kelly asserted.

"But I soon learned that what I had to do was to get into the Word. Accepting Christ is one thing but you must feed your spiritual body as you would feed your physical body."

Kelly developed spiritually as he launched into Bible studies. "After about eight months, the Bible became so illuminating," he shared. "I was understanding God, as the Word revealed what faith was all about. No longer did I want to go out into the streets and party. No longer did I want to hang out with the women and the drinking and all the lustful things the world has to offer."

Instead, Kelly found satisfaction in the Bible and in fellowship with Christians. He found joy in sharing Jesus Christ with his family, including his brother LeRoy, a former All-Star running back for the Cleveland Browns and twice the National Football League's leading rusher. Instead of the worldly temptations, he sought the Word.

"The more I read, the more I praised God, because I was lost," Kelly said. "I was a lost sinner but I can say I was lost but now I have been found. I was blind, but now I can see."

Kelly noted that Jesus can turn anyone's life from the realm of the lost to the family of the found. "God," Kelly frequently shares with teammates, "wants to deal with us where we are. And He shows the path to growth through Scripture, implanting His word into our hearts and minds."

The limelight surrounding baseball can make humility difficult. The practice of thinking "I did it" can overwhelm players.

"For many of us, that's a problem," Kelly said. "We think we've done it. But we haven't. And I haven't. I am a sinner saved by the grace of God. He said His grace is sufficient, so I take credit for nothing, but lift the glory to God. I do everything to glorify Him. He has allowed me to do this because He has humbled me."

Kelly views his role as recorded in the Bible, "You younger men, follow the leadership of those who are older. And all of you serve each other with humble spirits, for God gives special blessings to those who are humble, but sets himself against those who are proud" (1 Pet. 5:5 TLB).

Kelly hopes his leadership can bring his teammates to Christ.

Pat, a native of Philadelphia, was raised in a Christian home. But he shared a misconception which traps many. He thought he would go to heaven because his parents were confessed Christians.

After learning more about the Lord, Kelly realized, I'm going to heaven because I have professed my faith and have claimed my salvation by believing in Jesus Christ. People say we're all children of God, but we're not. He says that to those who receive Him, to them He gives the power to be called the sons of God. I know the reason I'm going to heaven is not because my mother will be there one day or because my father is there."

Reflecting on the glamour associated with baseball, Kelly paused, then said, forcefully, "I look back and I thank God that He brought me to the realization that glamour is not what life is all about. People die trying to achieve things here on this earth. People go off the deep end because they idolize worldly things. God said to seek Him first."

Ken Singleton came off a successful season— 1977—but was restless. He had belted 24 homers, drove in 99 and hit .328 but still he felt empty. His life seemed without direction.

"I felt I was doing my job well, but there was something missing," recalled Singleton, who came to Baltimore from Montreal in a 1975 trade. He started his career with the New York Mets.

That "something" for both Singleton and his wife, Colette, was Jesus Christ.

"The solace I find now is something to behold," Singleton shared. "It's an unbelievable feeling to know you have someone who you can really rely on. And on a personal note, I talk with my wife a lot more and we get along much better. We talk more about almost everything— not just baseball, but about things she does around the house. We had always gotten along well before, but we get along even better now because of our faith in the Lord."

Releasing the pressures of baseball to the Lord enables Singleton to focus on his performance without worrying about it.

"People tend to make too big a thing of baseball players," he said. "It's good to entertain these folks, but you shouldn't let this game go to your head and make you think you're ten steps beyond them. Baseball is just my job. The Lord has given me talent to play and I'm grateful for that."

Kelly and Singleton draw players who are searching. One of them is Billy Smith, signed by the Orioles as a free agent in 1977, after more than six years with the California Angels. Most of these years were spent in the minors. Eager to play, Smith eyed Baltimore as a team which would better utilize his abilities.

"When I came to Baltimore, I listened to Pat Kelly talk about his faith," Smith said. "As I listened to him, I started to ask him questions. He explained things to me and helped me considerably."

Ultimately, Smith asked Jesus to come into his heart. Now, he too has released the anxiety which had accumulated inside of him. "If He wants me to do well in this game, it will happen," said Smith. "If not, then I don't have to worry about it. That's a relief."

Players without faith on the Boston Red Sox

suffered painfully over the team's squandering a fourteen-game division lead to the New York Yankees in 1978 to lose a pennant they seemingly had won.

Along with a celebrated tea party that occurred two centuries ago, the Red Sox have helped to make Boston famous. Their fans are loyal, rooting for their summertime heroes during thick and thin. The intimacy of Fenway Park brings a sense of community between the players and fans. Though winners of only three American League titles since 1946, the Red Sox draw large crowds.

The 1979 season began as expected—the Sox, Yankees, Brewers and Orioles each entered the campaign as contenders, not pretenders.

When four teams vie for a title, nearly every game carries pressure. Players fight a complacency that any particular loss won't make a difference—because in the A.L. East, a single game can mark the difference between a championship and a bridesmaid. Boston knew that all too well, having finished one game behind New York in 1978.

So when Boston invaded the West Coast in July for a series with the Oakland A's, the Red Sox didn't take the A's lightly, despite Oakland's dismal record.

Jack Brohamer is to Boston what Pat Kelly is to Baltimore. He's a veteran, and a strong Christian. He looks to share his faith as well as his sports abilities.

Brohamer's conversion, though, was more traumatic.

After admittedly "fence-straddling" for several years, Brohamer came to the Lord in the aftermath of a tragic fire in 1977 which claimed the lives of three of his sister-in-law's children in Chicago. The emotion-torn parents were Christians. In a time of sorrow, they uplifted the Brohamers.

"Their faith is what brought them through the tragedy," Brohamer recalled. "Helene (his wife) and I saw something in their lives that we wanted. So we invited Jesus to enter our lives. We were thinking of doing it earlier, but we never seemed to go all the way. With the tragedy—the death of the children—we became Christians." It doesn't take a tragedy for other "fence-straddlers" to come to the Lord. It takes an invitation. Jesus accepts us for our wanderings, our searchings, our questions. He forgives us for our sins.

A fellowship with Jesus replaced the doubt for Jack Brohamer. It can for others too.

The fellowship, though, doesn't always produce instant results. Americans look for instant answers. Jim Wright, a promising Red Sox hurler, knows that. Working diligently for nine years to fulfill a dream is only part of Wright's inspiration. He climbed to the big leagues in 1978 and posted an 8-4 record, including a shutout in his first major-league start.

Wright's inspiration is his faith in Jesus. It is a faith which loved Jesus when it appeared that the major leagues were elusive; a faith which didn't slide because God's timetable was longer than his; a faith which praised God for a 1-10 record in Pawtucket as well as for finally making the big leagues.

"I think that anybody who has played this game knows you can get into some really bad times, and it's easy to get down on yourself," Wright said, pausing to catch his breath after wind sprints. "If you turn to Him and let Him lead you, He can take you through anything. It may seem like a crisis, but God can pull you through."

Wright credits chapel services in the minor leagues for developing his faith, making it more of a commitment and a life style. Delving into God's Word to learn about forgiveness and salvation helped Wright learn there is a purpose for his life.

And he learned there is a purpose for staying in the minor leagues nine years!

Steve Renko, a surprising performer for the Red Sox's dismantled pitching corps in 1979, also calls on God to direct his life. A lifelong believer, Renko is married to a preacher's daughter.

Renko, who played for Montreal for seven seasons before a 1975 trade to the Chicago Cubs, still has his Bible as a steady companion on the road. He never tires of the Lord's Word— or His strength.

During the off-season, Renko believes in the Bible's call for a faith that works. He is active with the Fellowship of Christian Athletes in Kansas City, speaking to youngsters for God and against drugs.

"It's important to teach kids that we handle the pressures and temptations of life through Jesus Christ," Renko said.

The message isn't controversial. It isn't going to be reported in the sports pages. It isn't going to earn a player a substantial endorsement fee.

But it will help change lives!

Playing on an expansion team like the Toronto Blue Jays can seem like the end of the line for a veteran player. It can seem like doom for a young player.

But to Rico Carty, it is another opportunity provided by the Lord to play baseball. And he doesn't take that opportunity lightly, even after sixteen springs.

Carty, the first player picked by Toronto when the Blue Jays were formed in 1977, has twice been traded, then reacquired. But Rico Carty is too busy to develop any inferiority complexes. He's been through much too much to get miffed over where he plays baseball.

Carty, born in 1941 in the Dominican Republic, started his career with the old Milwaukee Braves. In 1964, he finished second in the Rookie of the Year derby, batting .330 with 22 homers and 88 RBIs. The award was captured by Philadelphia's Dick Allen. Carty enjoyed four more successful seasons before he was struck with tuberculosis, forcing him to sit out more than a full season, including all of 1968.

Carty didn't wallow in self-pity. He didn't ask why. Simply but confidently he prayed, "Lord, help me to come back."

And back he came! Carty paced the Braves to the Western Division Title in 1969, batting .342 despite missing several games because of three repeated shoulder separations. He followed up in 1970 with a .366 average to win the National League batting crown. But in the off-season, adversity struck again. Playing winter ball in his homeland, Carty tore ligaments and cartilage in his knee. Surgery put him on the bench for all of 1971.

Again, Carty prayed for God's will in his life. "He helps you overcome a lot of frustration," Carty said. "With the help of God, I always knew I could come back."

Carty in 1979 maintained his lifetime batting average of over .300, put his career homer mark over 200, and his hits near 1,700. But one thing remained the same as when he was a rookie back in 1964. His companion on the road was his Bible.

Al Woods, a promising young outfielder for the Blue Jays, made his major-league debut in a Toronto uniform in the team's first game in 1977. In his first time at bat, Woods clubbed a home run. He finished the season with six homers and a respectable .284 batting average. His career looked bright.

But after a slow start in 1978, Toronto sent Woods back to the minor leagues. Without his faith in Jesus, Woods might have questioned his own abilities to play in the big leagues if an expansion team was giving up on him.

He gave the burden to Jesus. "Not to Al Woods," said Al Woods.

In 1979, Woods stuck with the Blue Jays, more polished after a season in the minors where he hit .313.

"You can win or lose, but it's not really a win-or-lose thing—it's what you give within yourself," Woods said of his faith and struggle to make the big leagues. "If you go out and give 100 percent and play hard, then you can lose and still be a winner. If you play like Jesus would expect you to play, the game is satisfying—regardless of what happens."

John Mayberry has tasted both victory and defeat. He came to Toronto in 1978 after seven seasons with the Kansas City Royals, including two in which the Royals won the Western Division of the American League, only to fall to the Yankees in the playoffs.

Raised by Christian parents in Detroit, Mayberry attended the same high school which produced major leaguers, Willie Horton and Alex Johnson.

Like a growing number of athletes, Mayberry spends his free time sharing the Lord with youngsters. "I tell them what Jesus is all about because I know they don't really understand who He is. So if I can just put a little bit into their heads, maybe they'll turn to Him."

Playing for an expansion team is an adjustment any time of the year. It was more so for Dyar Miller, traded from the high-flying California Angels in June of 1979 to the Blue Jays. He went from first place to last place.

Miller, though, appreciates his chance to play baseball, so he didn't complain. He played seven seasons in the minors before the Baltimore Orioles used him as a relief pitcher for three years before trading him to California in 1977.

"I think everything is in God's hands and baseball means a lot to me, but it's not the only thing," Miller said. "I think your relationship with God should be number one. I have good days even on my bad days because every day with God is a good day."

chapter ten

In this sports-craving world, soccer is king in Europe, football and baseball are national pastimes in America, and ice hockey is the leading sport in Canada.

But don't sell that too hard in Montreal, the home of the surprising Expos. Baseball took a gamble in 1969 by expanding across the border. Would fans accustomed to the fast pace of hockey be attracted to the more repetitious nature of baseball?

Yes! After eleven seasons, the Expos have averaged nearly 1.2 million fans per season. They began in crammed Garry Park, then moved into the expansive, new Olympic Stadium.

Expo fans in 1979 were like the Mets fans of a decade earlier. Their patience with an expansion team was growing thin. It was time for a winner!

One who gave fans plenty to cheer about is Gary Carter, baseball's premier young catcher.

But success doesn't spoil Carter. His faith in Jesus Christ keeps him humble—and thankful.

Carter, a native of Culver City, California, lost his mother to leukemia when he was twelve years old. It was then that he heard the Lord calling him.

But like many youngsters who are devoured by the worldly standard of status, Gary drifted from his faith at Sunny Hills High School in Fullerton, California. He was an honor student as well as a gifted athlete in baseball, basketball and football. He signed with the Expos out of high school.

After parts of three years in the minors, Carter climbed to the big leagues in 1974, at the tender age of twenty, and smashed eleven hits in twenty-seven at-bats in the closing days. The display earned him an invitation to spring training in 1975, where Carter met John Boccabella, a veteran catcher who taught Gary about the game—and about Jesus Christ.

"It wasn't until I met John and talked with him that I realized the Lord was the only one who really was going to guide me," Carter recalled. He and Boccabella became roommates. A short time later, Gary surrendered his life to Jesus—permanently.

Boccabella, at the twilight of his career, was as interested in helping Carter grow spiritually as he was with salvaging another season or two in baseball. Boccabella put his faith in the Lord, and was one of baseball's first outgoing Christians. Boccabella today is a frequent speaker at Baseball Chapel services around the country.

That 1975 season earned Carter the prestigious *Sporting News* Rookie of the Year award. He was runner-up to John Montefusco of San Franscisco for the Baseball Writer's Association version of the honor. Carter hit .270 with 17 homers.

Reflecting on it in an interview, Carter asserted, "I really owe it all to the Lord. I've had my ups and downs just like everyone else, but I feel that everything happens for a reason."

Carter suffered the jinx of the sophomore slump in 1976, batting just .219 with six home runs. But his faith held steadfast. He didn't doubt God.

"God was there to listen during the rough times," Carter said. He noted that the Bible warns about trying times. It says, "We can rejoice, too, when we run into problems and trials for we know that they are good for us— they help us learn to be patient. And patience develops strength of character in us and helps us trust God more each time we use it until finally our faith and hope are strong and steady" (Rom 5:3, 4 TLB).

Carter's patience produced a sensational

season in 1977, featuring 30 homers and a .284 batting average. He entered the 1979 season with the most home runs, 75, for an active player of his age.

But Carter wasn't heady. He knew the source of his strength.

"It really changes your life when you know Christ is in you," Carter noted. "I'm growing more and more every day. And I'm learning more and more how to walk my talk. With the pressures of baseball, it's relaxing to be able to go back to my room and have a short time just between myself and the Lord."

Shortstop Chris Speier has grown in the Lord. He shared how he tasted the sinful pleasures of life before he experienced true happiness through a personal relationship with Jesus Christ.

Like Carter, Speier reached the major leagues at the early age of twenty, as the starting shortstop for the San Francisco Giants in 1971. He played just one season in the minor leagues.

A native of Alameda, California, an Oakland suburb, Speier was a prep standout in both baseball and basketball. The Giants drafted him after his freshman season at the University of California at Santa Barbara. His quick elevation to the major leagues motivated him "to try to experience everything in life in one year. Probably most of the things I experienced were on the negative side of our life style."

But at age twenty-two, Speier found a wife—and the Lord. His wife, Aleta, was a strong Christian. Her influence guided Chris to the Lord.

"My life made a complete turnaround," said Speier. "The Lord has changed my life to make it completely new each day, and I offer every day up to the Lord."

His conversion occurred at about the same time Baseball Chapel originated, and he has seen its influence in the spiritual lives of baseball players.

"I don't let the past or times when I fail bother me," Speier said. "I know that the Lord is a forgiving Father. It's new and exciting every day to just open your heart to His will. I don't look too far ahead or behind any more. I take one day at a time, thankful to the Lord for it and the life style that He's given me."

Speier noted the Bible passage which aptly describes what happened to him. It says, "When someone becomes a Christian he becomes a brand new person inside. He is not the same any more. A new life has begun!" (2 Cor. 5:17 TLB).

San Francisco baseball fans are among the most unloyal in the nation, turning their plaudits to condemnation quicker than most.

Speier batted consistently from 1972 to 1975

and played the infield better than most in his position, earning a spot on the All-Star team for three of those four years. But 1976 was an off-season—.266—and Giant fans promptly let Speier know about it.

Reflecting on that period, he asserted, "The pressures of the game are ones that can get you down at times. But Jesus is happy with us if we play at 100 percent and give our best in each game. If we win or lose doesn't really matter. I think we're always a winner in His eyes."

The Giants traded Speier to Montreal a month into the 1977 season. He, Aleta and their three children make Ste. Adele, Quebec, their home. During the off-season, Speier is a busy messenger for Jesus Christ.

He practices the Bible admonition, "Dear brothers, what's the use of saying that you have faith and are Christians if you aren't proving it by helping others?" (James 2:14 TLB).

Helping others gives Chris Speier more satisfaction than a game-winning hit. He is active with the Right-to-Life Movement. He talked with every National League club about the abortion issue, and won 110 supporters to form a group called Athletes for Life.

"I try to offer each game for the Lord with a special intention, such as for all the unborn babies," Speier said. He and Aleta also teach confirmation classes to youngsters and talk with engaged couples about how to let God manage their marriages.

"There are a lot of things you can do as a Christian," Speier offered. "The doors are wide open, and it's a fulfilling life. I find more satisfaction outside of baseball."

So does Jim Mason, a utility infielder for the Expos who once hit a home run in a World Series when he played for the New York Yankees in 1976.

A native of Mobile, Alabama, playing baseball was Mason's desire from the time he pitched a perfect game in an Alabama State Babe Ruth Tournament. Born in 1950, he was drafted out of the University of South Alabama by the Texas Rangers in 1968. After five minor-league seasons, Jim stuck with the Rangers in 1973, but was traded to the Yankees, where he played for three seasons before the Toronto Blue Jays expansion club drafted him in 1977.

But after only twenty-two games, Toronto traded Jim back to Texas, where he played for two seasons before Montreal acquired him in an off-season trade in 1978.

Like several professional athletes, Mason discovered that trying to manage his own life was as difficult as running up ice in a snowstorm. Just when you think you're making progress, you slip backwards. Entering the 1977 season, Jim became introspective. "As I examined my life, I thought it was on my own that I had reached my accomplishments," he recalled. "I always wanted to play for the Yankees, and I did. I always wanted to play in the World Series, and I did. I wanted to hit a home run in the World Series, and I did. It got to the point where I said to myself, 'Is this all there is to life?' It came down to that. I thought that there's got to be more to life than this."

And he discovered that there is.

"I had a void," Jim recalled. "I was just living from day to day without any purpose in life."

Jesus Christ filled that void—and gave him renewed purpose.

"It's made my life so much easier because I can turn my life over to someone who knows how to handle it," Mason explained. "I was trying to run my life all those years with all those burdens and worries. But now I turn them over to Jesus, knowing He will take care of them."

Mason said he had fooled himself for several years. "I thought I had been a Christian all of those years but I guess I was just fooling myself. You can't burn the rope on both ends—you have to be either a Christian or not one. When I accepted Christ, I found out what being a Christian really means."

For Mason, it means a better family life.

"Our marriage is better," he shared. "We

understand each other better. We don't argue any more. We're bringing our children up in the church. You can't really appreciate how much change we've had in our lives since I accepted Christ."

Living a Christian life means relinquishing habits and life styles which are contradictory to Jesus' example.

"You're going to have to give up things," Mason noted. "You think those things are tough for you to give up now, but after you give them up, you see that you really didn't need them anyway."

Another feature of his conversion is the Lord's grace in helping him face temptations. "I think the toughest part of baseball is the night life. You're on the road a lot, away from home, and if you have to endure on your own, it's tough. But asking God for the power to endure, enables you to do it. You can't do it on your own."

Andre Dawson, one of the Expos' three talented young outfielders, once tried to do it on his own but discovered a better way—through Jesus Christ.

Dawson, born in 1954 in Miami, garnered the 1977 Rookie of the Year awards from both the baseball writers and *The Sporting News*, hitting .282 with 19 home runs. Drafted by the Expos out of Florida A&M in 1975, Dawson played minor-league ball for only portions of two season, impressing management with his speed, power and defense.

After breaking Steve Garvey's Pioneer League record for total bases in 1975 and leading the league in six offensive categories, Dawson skipped from the Rookie League to Double-A ball at Quebec to start the 1976 season. But after 40 games, boasting a .347 average with eight home runs, he was called up to Denver of the Triple-A Association, where he hit .350 with 20 homers in seventy-four games. Denver won the championship and Dawson won an invitation to the big leagues.

He, Ellis Valentine and Warren Cromartie gave Montreal the youngest and most talented outfield in the major leagues.

Though baptized as a youngster, Dawson's personal commitment to Jesus paralleled the beginning of his baseball career in 1975.

"I used to have quite a few fears and I was tense and nervous," Dawson recalled. "At that time I asked the Lord to take these fears out of my life and to teach me to be more at ease. He did all this for me."

Despite a sophomore season which produced a .253 batting average with twenty-five homers and seventy-two RBIs, Dawson said he struggled.

"I started off slowly but I didn't give up at any time," he explained. "I always knew it was just a matter of time. I realized that all I can do is try to go out and play to the best of my ability. If it's His will for me to be successful, then I will be. God runs everything. That's an advantage for a Christian player. He knows the Lord is always there and always will be."

And that includes baseball games in Canada!

There was a time when Sal Bando leaned only on Sal Bando. The fruits of victory were his. The frustrations of defeat were dealt to scapegoats.

But that's the "old" Sal Bando—the one who climbed to national prominence on the World Champion Oakland A's from 1972 to 1974 and the one who tasted athletic glory but still searched for contentment.

Bando was among the contingent in Oakland who came to faith or renewed faith in Jesus Christ after the banner years. Bando is among those players touched by former manager Alvin Dark. And, in turn, Bando shared his enthusiasm for the Lord with Gene Tenace.

Now at the twilight of his career with the Milwaukee Brewers, Bando was at his happiest. The Brewers are one of baseball's most improved teams but Bando's contentment isn't tied to wins and losses any more. It's derived from his steady relationship with God.

Bando's 1979 season was sluggish, a drop

from his seventeen homers and .285 average in 1978. The "old" Sal might have absorbed the pressure. He would have leaned on Sal. But now, as Bando puts it, "I have Christ to lean on."

Bando, a cheerful, easygoing third baseman, signed for a reported $30,000 bonus out of Arizona State in 1965 with the Kansas City A's. His first full season in the major leagues was in 1968, the A's first year in Oakland.

He gained national attention in 1969 by slugging thirty-one home runs and hitting .281 for a developing Oakland team. By 1975, Bando had fame, three world championship rings, All-Star honors, and monetary security. But he was out of fellowship with the Lord. Dark's influence in 1974 and 1975 prompted Bando to rededicate his life to Jesus in August of 1975.

"Ever since then, I've tried to grow and work at becoming a strong Christian," Bando said.

"Growth is not an option but an essential," popular Christian speaker Howard Hendricks frequently tells conferences. Hendricks is a seminary professor and spiritual adviser to several professional athletes.

"I was struggling in baseball at the time," Bando recalled in an interview. "It was then that I began to see that baseball was consuming too much of my life. I had always had faith, having been raised a Catholic, but it wasn't until 1975, after talking with Alvin, that my faith was revived."

Like a score of athletes in the 1970s, Bando's revival prompted him to change his priorities. "I'm being loving to those I might not be too crazy about," Bando said. He noted the Bible's repeated admonition to love.

A stereotype in sports assumes athletes guzzle beer or promote their careers during free time. But for Bando, his rededication also altered how he utilizes his leisure time.

"I think any free time my wife and I have we spend studying the Bible, going to studies, and praying," said Bando. "Everything revolves around Christ. If we have a problem, we pray to the Lord. We lift it to Him."

Bando believes in the Bible admonition, "Now that you realize how kind the Lord has been to you. . . . Long to grow up into the fullness of your salvation; cry for this as a baby cries for his milk" (1 Pet. 2:2,3 TLB).

Another "baby Christian" eager for the "Lord's milk" is Paul Molitor, an equally enthusiastic Brewer whose growth as a Christian parallels his development on the field. Molitor was one of baseball's top hitters in 1979.

Born in 1956 in St. Paul, Minnesota, Molitor dreamed about playing baseball long before he knew what a double-play pivot entailed. A gifted schoolboy athlete, he attended the University of Minnesota until the Brewers drafted him in 1977. He played in just 64 minor-league games before he impressed management with his readiness to hit and field in the big leagues.

Molitor's association with baseball brought him in touch with his faith.

"The spring of 1977 was a tough one for me in college ball," he recalled, sharing his testimony in the Brewer dugout. "I had a couple of friends who were Christians. I decided I needed to make a commitment because some aspects of my life were headed in the wrong direction."

Molitor accepted Christ as his Savior to let Him help change his life style.

"Before I was a Christian I was the party type, and the type that when things were going bad I would turn to heavy drinking," Molitor recalled. "But now when I'm down or depressed, I know I've got the Word of God to go to for strength."

The Bible puts it like this: "Wicked men trust themselves alone, and fail; but the righteous man trusts in me, and lives!" (Hab. 2:4 TLB).

Molitor asserted, "Before I came to faith, I was either in a good mood or in a bad mood. Now I'm learning to be a happy person because I know that I have Christ in my life. I have everlasting life as His commitment to me."

Eternal life is God's gift to all believers. It doesn't take a .300 batting average. It doesn't take 30 home runs. It doesn't take a flawless life. It takes faith. It takes faith in Jesus Christ as Lord and Savior.

The Bible explains, "God has shown us a different way to heaven—not by 'being good enough' and trying to keep his laws, but by a new way (though, not new, really, for the Scriptures told about it long ago). Now God says he will accept and acquit us—declare us 'not guilty'—if we trust Jesus Christ to take away our sins. And we all can be saved in this same way, by coming to Christ, no matter who we are or what we have been like" (Rom. 3:21, 22 TLB).

Matching the growth of Christian baseball players is the curiosity and acceptance of nonbelieving teammates.

"There was a time when I wasn't a Christian that I really looked down on some of the Christians on my college team," Molitor said. "But now I think Christian beliefs are more widely accepted. Our club is very, very comfortable."

Molitor notices a difference in how Christian players react to situations in baseball.

"I know I have greater self-control," he said. "And I can see that the Christians on our team are the most happy people. They can deal with failure a lot better."

Molitor, who batted .272 during his rookie

season in 1978 to finish third in the "Rookie of the Year" derby, looks at baseball like this:

"The most satisfying thing in my life is the ability to give my baseball life over to Christ. I can go out there and play at my best whether we're in Oakland playing before 500 fans or in front of 50,000 in Milwaukee. I know that my only guidance really comes from Christ. That helps me to be consistent."

It's the same lesson San Bando learned when he learned not to lean on Sal any more—but on Jesus Christ.

The self-imposed pressure to make it to the major leagues can put the rest of life's events out of perspective. The desire to excel and to be among the elite 650 men to play baseball can be awesome.

It was thus for John Anthony Castino, a twenty-two-year-old who didn't expect his dream to be achieved so quickly. Castino plays third base for the Minnesota Twins, one of the surprise clubs of 1979. Castino and Alfredo Griffin of Toronto were co-Rookie of the Year in the American League for 1979.

Castino first grabbed the attention of Minnesota scouts when his Rollins College (Illinois) freshman baseball team played an exhibition game with the Twins in 1974. Castino impressed the scouts with his talent at the plate and in the field with his flashy, flawless defense. Two years later, the Twins picked him third in the free-agent draft. His minor-league career, though brief, was life-altering. This was not because he bypassed Triple-A ball, but because he had a concerned teammate in Double-A ball.

"I was in Melbourne, Florida, at the minor-league spring training camp when I had a yearning for something more in life, something beyond a career or a family," Castino recalled. "I knew there was something more important to life. A friend introduced me to Christianity and I began to study and read the Bible. Things suddenly fell into place for me. For the first time, everything seemed to make perfect sense. Believing in Jesus was the best thing that ever happened to me."

Castino's baseball ability and faith both developed rapidly. In his third season of minor-league baseball, at Orlando, Florida, Castino was picked for the Southern League All-Star team and led the league in fielding from his third-base position. He also hit .275 and earned an invitation to spring training from manager Gene Mauch.

"My faith has helped me with the need for consistency in my life," Castino shared while sitting in the dugout before a game. "It has helped me during low areas of my career. I've had some bad times, but Christianity lifts me from despair. Believing in Christ has been a steppingstone for me in bolstering my faith in myself and in God."

Castino delights in sharing his faith with fans—and he does it in a manner similar to Jerry Terrell of the Royals. When asked to sign his autograph on anything other than a baseball, Castino affixes his name plus a favorite Scripture verse, such as Romans 8:28 or John 3:16.

John 3:16 is one of the hallmarks of Christianity: "For God loved the world so much that he gave his only Son so that anyone who believes in him shall not perish but have eternal life" (TLB).

Christian athletes can do more than sign Bible verses to help counter their playboy images that have been created by the secular media.

"Whether we're having a bad time or a good time, a Christian ballplayer can be consistent in his attitude," Castino said. "He can have a humble understanding of who he really is and what he is on this earth for, and to realize that life offers ups and downs. But most important, a Christian ballplayer—or any Christian—can know the priorities of life and know that God always comes first."

Putting priorities into perspective became easier for Twins second-baseman, Bobby Randall, after his conversion in 1977. It also enabled him to accept manager Mauch's plans to platoon him in 1979. Randall, a native of Norton, Kansas, was an accomplished major-leaguer when he noticed how his Christian teammates and friends seemed to live such contented lives.

"I began seeing the reality of Christianity in other believers' lives and realized that worldly things weren't giving me the things that were of value in life," Randall recalled. "I saw from people who I thought had the true value in their lives that the power came from the Lord. It was at that point that I realized my faith in Jesus."

He noted that everyone is free to choose to draw upon Christ's power. It is like having an electric shaver. Until one decides to plug it into an electrical outlet, it has no power. It is the same in many of our lives. It was the same in Bobby Randall's life.

"On the field my faith helps me, like it says in Romans 8:28, to realize that everything works to the glory of God, and that all things work for good for those who love God. This means I can play the best I can play and know I don't have to worry about the results. But I also believe it is the same off the field, away from baseball."

As the season unfolded, Randall had reason to be disappointed. After three seasons as a starter, he was ticketed for part-time duty. But in his eyes, there are no part-timers in God's kingdom.

Randall deftly fielded the question of whether

Christian athletes can counter the playboy, selfish image of ballplayers that is painted in the secular media.

"Talk is cheap," Bobby said. "Paraphrasing Proverbs, what a man says is not nearly as important as what a man does. It's easy to talk with writers and to give them what they want to hear. But I think it's the player's life style more than anything else which fans remember. I think it's difficult for anyone to sit in the stands and say, 'I want to pattern my life after this guy,' or to read something in the newspaper and conclude, 'I want to pattern my life after this guy.' What you read and what you see are not always the truth, especially on the ball field. Some guys have a certain image that looks very appealing but maybe they're projecting a life which they don't actually live."

Veteran pitcher Jerry Koosman hasn't had to worry about his image for more than a decade.

Koosman, a native of Appleton, Minnesota, had a homecoming in 1979 after twelve colorful seasons with the New York Mets, which included three World Series wins and an overall National League record of 140 wins and 137 losses.

Even after a dozen springs, Koosman was excited about baseball—and about sharing his faith. Christianity has been part of his life as long as his Minnesota heritage. He credits his faith for enduring the pinnacle of World Series success to the doldrums of a 20-defeat season.

"My faith gives me a lot of confidence in myself," Koosman said. "The Lord will provide whether it's solving your problems or not. I feel that He created me to play this game as long as I can, the best way I can, and He doesn't care if I win or lose or whether the next Christian wins or loses. The main thing is to go out there and do what He created you for, and to do your best."

Koosman yearns to improve his ability to share his faith with teammates and friends.

"Sometimes I haven't been able to always have the right words at the right times to answer some of the questions that are asked or the statements that are made," he said. "That upsets me. I'm not a gifted man with words. Sometimes I go back to my room and think about something that was asked and think of an answer which I could have given. I think that God says to ballplayers, as He says to all Christians, to go and preach His Word. This I try to do."

So does Dave Goltz, an ex-Twins hurler. Goltz is like many Christian athletes. His prayers seek God's will, not his own.

"Saying a little prayer before each game relaxes me," said Goltz, the Twins' starting day pitcher in 1979. "I never ask for too much, just for the ability to do the best I can. It gives me a relaxing feeling to know I've got somebody whom I can talk with. Off the field, my faith enables me to enjoy life as it is, not trying to go out and look for the elusive something special, but to just enjoy what is there."

Geoff Zahn enjoys life as it is. But it hasn't always been that way. Zahn, who enjoyed his best American League season in 1979, was the Twins' chaplain, and one of the game's most devout players.

He shared several aspects of faith and baseball.

"As baseball players, we are in all types of temptations, but the rewards of obeying God's laws and staying in Scripture are beyond the rewards of giving in to temptation," Zahn said in an interview. "I find that when I get out of God's Word, I fall into temptation, then I feel just terrible. I long to get back into the Word and to confess my sins. The rewards and peace which follow are fantastic."

Zahn's personal walk with Jesus began in 1972 in Albuquerque, New Mexico, when he played on a Los Angeles Dodgers Triple-A club. A teammate, Bill Ralston, invited Geoff to share a Bible study in the Book of Romans.

"It was then I realized I couldn't get into heaven or receive eternal life through good works," Zahn recalled. "I had been trying because I felt that as long as I was a good person and born in America and was a Christian, I was going to heaven."

But Zahn learned that he had been fooling himself.

"I had been trying to please my own ego," he continued. "I had to realize I couldn't do anything but accept what God had already done for me by sending His Son, Jesus Christ."

The Christian life is a continuous walk to seek and follow God's will. The power of the Holy Spirit is an active part of the walk.

"I don't believe you just get zapped into Christianity," Zahn asserted. "When you look at the Beatitudes and the theme of the New Testament, you see that the Christian experience is a day-by-day walk and maturing with the Lord. The more you're into the Word, the more you know what God has in store for you. I feel that you come into the body of believers at one particular time but it is a day-by-day maturing."

Baseball players, by society's standards, are recognized as successes.

"But that doesn't necessarily mean we're successful in God's eyes just because we're successful in society's eyes," Zahn said. "I think a lot of people tend to listen to us and think, 'I can become a Christian and be successful too.' I struggle with that correlation."

As if summing up the essential lesson learned by a growing number of players coming to the

Lord, Zahn said:

"My faith helps me to keep a balance and to have a standard for life. A life without Christ is dead in sin. The Lord has chosen me and because I have made a decision to follow Him, the Bible proclaims that I—and all others who similarly follow—will have eternal life. For me, that is the essence of life. So it's not whether my faith helps me as a baseball player or whether it's a good luck charm or anything like that—it gives me a standard and a continuity for my life.

"Playing baseball is an occupation, not an excuse for an athlete to become a six-month Christian."

It is clear that America's major-league baseball players who proclaim Jesus Christ as their Lord and Savior strive to be full-time Christians. This is what happens when faith steals home!

SUGGESTED READING